ABC of Egyptian Hieroglyphs

Jaromir Malek

With illustrations and hieroglyphs by
Marion Cox

Ashmolean Museum, Oxford
1998

Contents

Introduction

Hieroglyphic script was used by the inhabitants of Egypt from its introduction in about 3000 BC until its last recorded instance in AD 394. Although hieroglyphs are pictures of people, animals, birds and various objects, they are not mere picture writing. In order to be able to read and understand a text written in Egyptian hieroglyphs, it is necessary to know how each sign was read (pronounced), and to know the language, Egyptian. Learning Egyptian is not different from trying to master a language which employs an unfamiliar script, such as Russian, Chinese, or Urdu.

This publication explains some of the rules of the hieroglyphic script and Egyptian language. You can take it to the Ashmolean Museum in Oxford and read it in front of the monuments described in it, but it is just as easy to use at home. We hope that it will encourage you to try to learn more about Egypt.

The branch of learning which is concerned with ancient Egypt is called Egyptology. Students reading Egyptology spend several years learning the language, and this small book cannot pretend to achieve the same result much more quickly. In particular, it does not attempt to penetrate the complex and difficult area of Egyptian grammar in sufficient depth to enable you to 'read' a text in the proper sense. To try to do so would turn this publication, intended for the ordinary museum visitor, into a specialized study. Grammatically, the texts offered for reading are fairly straightforward; difficult features are explained but some have to be taken on trust. The book may provide a sufficient stimulus for some of you to take up Egyptian more seriously. Those who do will find a list of useful publications on page 48.

ABC of Egyptian Hieroglyphs started as two lectures given by Jaromir Malek for young members of the Ashmole Club in the Ashmolean Museum in Oxford. We are grateful to Lady Sykes, Dr. P.R.S. Moorey, and Mr Ian Charlton for their support then and now. It gives us pleasure to acknowledge help received from Dr. Helen Whitehouse, Dr. Diana Magee, Dr. Jane Jakeman and Miss Elizabeth Miles, and to thank Mr. Andrew Ivett for the patience and care taken over the design of this book.

All the monuments described and illustrated on pages 16-47 are in the Ashmolean Museum.

Jaromir Malek is editor of *Topographical Bibliography of Ancient Egyptian Hieroglyphic Texts, Reliefs, and Paintings* and Keeper of the Archive at the Griffith Institute, Ashmolean Museum, Oxford.

Marion Cox specializes in archaeological drawings. She has illustrated many books and articles on ancient civilizations and drawn hieroglyphs for a number of Egyptological publications.

Chronology of Egyptian history

Egyptian history is usually divided into several 'kingdoms' and thirty or thirty-one royal dynasties (groups of kings). This publication uses BC and AD dates, but the following table will provide a guide to the dating of monuments described on museum labels in a more traditional way.

Ancient Egypt	
The Predynastic period (includes Dynasty 0)	*c*.5000-2950 BC
The Early Dynastic period (Dynasties 1-2)	*c*.2950-2647 BC
The Old Kingdom (Dynasties 3-8)	2647-2124 BC
The First Intermediate period (Dynasties 9, 10 and first part of Dynasty 11)	2123-*c*.2040 BC
The Middle Kingdom (second part of Dynasty 11 and Dynasties 12 and 13)	*c*.2040-1648 BC
The Second Intermediate period (Dynasties 14-17)	1648-1540 BC
The New Kingdom (Dynasties 18-20)	1540-1069 BC
The Third Intermediate period (Dynasties 21-24)	1069-*c*.715 BC
The Late period (Dynasties 25-31)	*c*.715-332 BC
Ptolemaic period	332-30 BC
Egypt as a Roman province	30 BC - AD 395
Byzantine Egypt	AD 395-642
Egypt conquered by the Arabs	AD 642

The decipherment of hieroglyphs

After Octavian's victory over the navy of Mark Antony and Queen Cleopatra VII at Actium in September 31 BC, Egypt became part of the Roman empire. During the centuries which followed there was a steady, though not abrupt, decline in the building of temples and tombs in which hieroglyphs were used. Ancient Egyptian religion was giving way to Christianity. The last known hieroglyphic text was inscribed in the temple at Philae, near Aswan at the southern border of Egypt, about four hundred years later, in AD 394. Some time after that, the knowledge of hieroglyphs was lost and remained so for nearly a millennium and a half.

Occasional references to hieroglyphs occurred in the works of inquisitive authors such as Horapollo, an Egyptian writer and philosopher of the late 5th century, and Ibn Wahshiyya, an Arab writer of the 10th century. European interest in Egyptian civilization and hieroglyphs was awakened during the Renaissance by scholars like Athanasius Kircher in the 17th century. Rome in particular contained a large number of inscribed Egyptian monuments taken there during the Roman occupation of Egypt. Several monuments brought from Egypt to this country in the 17th century are in the Ashmolean Museum, and include the stela of the priest Sheri from Saqqara (see pages 16-17).

The main obstacle to the rediscovery of the understanding of hieroglyphs was the mistaken idea that they were symbols or picture writing, not a systematic writing system. The decisive help with the decipherment was provided by the discovery of a text recorded in three different scripts (hieroglyphic, Demotic, and Greek) at Rosetta (El-Rashid, in the north-western Delta). This was in 1799, during Napoleon's invasion of Egypt. The text, on a large basalt slab, is a copy of a decree issued in 196 BC in honour of king Ptolemy V Epiphanes. The monument, known as the Rosetta Stone, is now in the British Museum.

Several scholars attempted to understand the hieroglyphic part of the text (they could, of course, read the Greek part easily and had some understanding of the Demotic text). One of them, the Englishman Thomas Young, came very close, but the fame of the decipherment deservedly belongs to the brilliant Frenchman Jean-François Champollion. The occurrence of the cartouches (oval frames) with the phonetically (using sound-signs, not symbols or picture-writing) written Greek name of king Ptolemy provided a vital point of departure in the intellectual journey of discovery which led him to similarly written groups of hieroglyphs in Egyptian names and words on other monuments. The final confirmation of the correctness of his method took place on 14 September, 1822. Gradually, it became once again possible to read hieroglyphic texts. Egyptology, the study of ancient Egypt, was established as a scholarly subject. Nowadays it is taught at universities in many parts of the world.

The Egyptian language

Egyptian was the main language of Egypt before the Arab conquest in AD 642. From then on its last form, called Coptic, was under increasing pressure from Arabic and eventually ceased to be spoken sometime in the 16th century. Nowadays, the version of Coptic which was used in northern Egypt ('Bohairic dialect') still survives as the liturgical language of the Coptic (Christian) Church. The spoken and written language of modern Egypt is Arabic which has its own script.

Egyptian belongs to the Afro-Asiatic (Hamito-Semitic) group of languages of north-eastern Africa and western Asia. These include Berber and some Ethiopian languages, ancient Akkadian, Aramaic, Hebrew, Arabic, and several other languages.

The Egyptian language was spoken and written during some 3000 years of pharaonic history, and for another 1500 years after the decline of ancient Egyptian civilization. It did not remain the same throughout this long period, and can be divided into several stages of development which differ in grammar and to some extent in vocabulary.

Archaic Egyptian.
Spoken before 2650 BC; few contemporary written records although later copies of certain religious texts probably retain some characteristics of this stage of Egyptian.

Old Egyptian.
Spoken and written 2650-2100 BC.

Middle (also called classical) Egyptian.
Spoken 2100-1550 BC, but written as the literary language of Egypt (one which had to be learnt in the same way we learn Latin) for the rest of Egyptian history.

Late Egyptian.
Spoken from 1550 BC onwards; used for written records from 1350 BC.

Demotic.
A successor of Late Egyptian written from 650 BC. The last Demotic text dates to AD 452.

Coptic.
A successor of Demotic, written from AD 250.

It is important to distinguish these stages of the development of Egyptian from different scripts.

The scripts

Egyptian was written in several different scripts and some of them were in use simultaneously. The number of Egyptian texts is the largest of any language in the ancient Near East. The texts range from administrative documents through literary works to religious and funerary compositions. This book concentrates on hieroglyphs, but a few words about the other writing methods are also necessary.

The hieroglyphic script.
Used for the writing of Archaic, Old, and Middle Egyptian.

This was introduced shortly before 3000 BC and continued to be used throughout Egyptian history. The hieroglyphs (from the Greek *hieros*, 'sacred', and *gluphe*, 'carving') were mostly employed for monumental inscriptions, often chiselled into stone or painted on objects made of wood or other materials. They were arranged in lines or columns, and could be read from right or left.

The hieratic script.
Used for the writing of Archaic, Old, Middle, and Late Egyptian.

The hieratic script (from the Greek *hieratikos*, 'priestly') appeared at about the same time as the hieroglyphs, and possibly even earlier. Both methods of writing are closely related. In most cases, hieratic signs can be recognized as cursive (simplified) counterparts of the more detailed hieroglyphs. The relationship is sometimes compared to that of our printed and handwritten texts, but the hieratic script continued to develop independently of hieroglyphs and evolved its own special rules. Hieratic was usually written in black or red ink with a reed brush, and came to be used mainly for administrative purposes (documents), and later for religious compositions. Hieratic inscriptions are usually on papyri or ostraca (potsherds or limestone flakes); those incised into stone or wood are rare. Hieratic was written in lines or columns, but was read only from right to left.

The Demotic script.
Used exclusively for the writing of Demotic (from the Greek *demotikos*, 'popular').

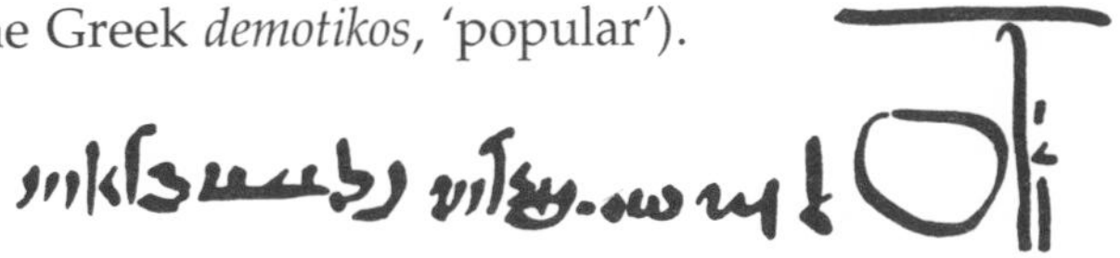

This script appeared with the new stage of the development of the language, Demotic, around 650 BC. It was mostly written with a reed brush, but instances of texts carved into stone (as on the Rosetta Stone, see page 5) are also known. Demotic was arranged in lines and was read from right to left.

The Coptic script.
Used exclusively for the writing of Coptic and closely linked to the spread of Christianity.

Coptic (from the Arabic *qibt* which, in its turn, derives from the Greek *Aiguptios*, 'Egyptian'), was written in Greek letters with several additional signs for special Egyptian sounds. The earliest Coptic texts date to about AD 250. Coptic was written in lines from left to right.

The direction of writing

Standard monumental inscriptions of pharaonic Egypt employed about seven hundred hieroglyphs, but there were also signs which differed only in details and others which were customized for special reasons. These proliferated enormously during the Ptolemaic period, after 332 BC. Modern computerized hieroglyphic fonts hold nearly 10,000 signs and the figure will, no doubt, continue to increase. A much smaller number of hieroglyphs, some two hundred and fifty, formed the core of the writing system and occurred frequently.

Hieroglyphic signs always remained recognizable representations of people, animals, birds, or various objects, and their close connection with reality was never lost. They are almost always coloured (although the colours may by now have faded or disappeared completely) and often display fine details. As the forms of depicted objects changed, so did the hieroglyphs.

On the walls of tombs and temples, or on monuments such as statues and stelae (stone tablets), hieroglyphs were neatly combined with the scenes and monuments to which they belonged. They were facing the same way as the human figures which they accompanied and filled the space around them as completely as possible. When inscribing hieroglyphs on monuments, it was important to maintain their correct mutual proportions and to avoid unsightly empty spaces. Whenever possible, signs were grouped into imaginary squares. This sometimes prompted the scribe to re-arrange their order, to tuck small signs into convenient space close to larger signs, or to turn low flat signs into tall narrow signs.

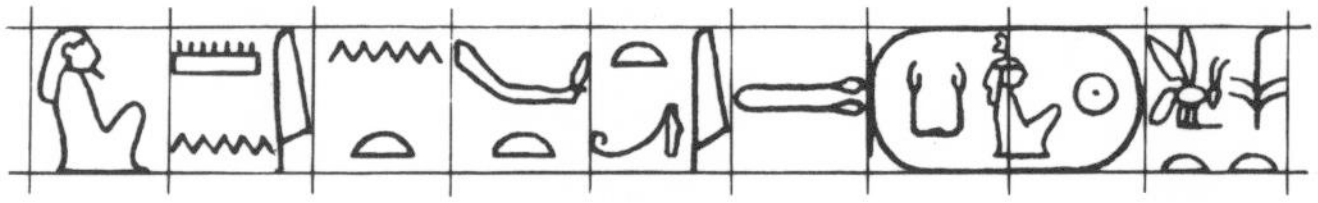

Hieroglyphs were written mainly from right to left, either in lines or in columns. Those showing people and animals always look (and birds point with their beaks) towards the beginning of the text.

If desired, hieroglyphs could also be written from left to right, again either in lines or in columns. The only direction which was not admissible was writing in columns starting at the bottom.

In this publication, hieroglyphs are always shown as they appear on the monument, and it is up to you to establish in which direction they should be read.

The most frequent hieroglyphic signs.

Part 1: The Egyptian alphabet

Vowels (such as our *a*, *e*, or *o*) were not written. There were twenty-four hieroglyphs for single consonants (or, to put it less accurately, single letters), plus several alternative signs. They are called uniliteral (alphabetic) signs and may be described as the Egyptian alphabet. In theory, any word could be written using just these signs.

In the list which follows, the signs are presented as they would appear in a text written from left to right. In a text written from right to left they would become their mirror images.

sign	how we transliterate (record) it	how we pronounce it	what it shows	sign	how we transliterate (record) it	how we pronounce it	what it shows
	*ꜣ*	*a	vulture		*ḥ*	*h	twisted flax
	*i͗*	*i (as in Nick)	flowering reed		*ḫ*	*kh	jar lid
 or 	*y*	*y (as Y in Yasmin)	two reeds/strokes		*ẖ*	*kh	animal's belly
	*ꜥ*	*a	forearm	 or	*s* (the latter formerly *z*)	*s (*z)	cloth/door-bolt
 or 	*w*	*w or u	quail chick		*š*	*sh	pool
	*b*	*b	lower leg		*q*	*k	hill slope
	*p*	*p	stool		*k*	*k	basket
	*f*	*f	horned viper		*g*	*g (as in Gary)	jar stand
 or 	*m*	*m	owl/ ?	 or 	*t*	*t	loaf/pestle
 or 	*n*	*n	water/crown		*ṯ*	*tj (as Ch in Charles)	tethering rope
	*r*	*r	mouth		*d*	*d	hand
	*h*	*h	courtyard		*ḏ*	*dj (as G in George)	cobra

Approximate pronunciation is indicated by an asterisk *. To be able to read groups of consonants, we insert short *e where necessary, so *snb* becomes *seneb. This is artificial; the precise pronunciation is often uncertain. Do not be confused by the fact that the suggested pronunciation of consonants *ꜣ*, *i͗* and *ꜥ*, which do not occur in English, is *a, *i and *a, our vowels!

The most frequent hieroglyphic signs.

Part 2: Biliteral signs

An important group of hieroglyphic signs represents combinations of two consonants. These are called biliteral signs. What the hieroglyphs depict has no connection with the meaning of the word in which they appear. Each sign simply conveys two sounds. In order to be able to pronounce some of these signs, insert *e where necessary.

ꜣw (*aw) part of a backbone
ꜣb (*ab) or mr (*mer) chisel
ꞽw (*iew) foal
ꞽm (*im) ?
ꞽn (*in) fish
ꞽr (*ir) eye
ꞽs (*is) bundle of reeds
ꜥꜣ (*aa) column
ꜥq (*ak) cormorant
ꜥḏ (*adj) needle with twine
wꜣ (*wa) lasso
wꜥ (*wa) harpoon
wp (*wep) horns
wn (*wen) hare
wn (*wen) flower
wr (*wer) sand-martin
wḏ (*wedj) cord on a stick
bꜣ (*ba) stork
bḥ (*beh) or ḥw (*hew) tusk

pꜣ (*pa) duck
pr (*per) house
pḥ (*peh) lion's hind-quarters
mꜣ (*ma) sickle
mꞽ (*mi) jug in a net
mꞽ (*mi) forearm holding a bowl
mw (*mew) ripples of water
mn (*men) draught-board
mr (*mer) or mꞽ (*mi) channel
mr (*mer) hoe
mḥ (*meh) whip
ms (*mes) animal skins
mt (*met) phallus
mt or mwt (*met or *mut) vulture
nꞽ (*ni) forearm
nw (*new) bowl
nw (*new) adze
nb (*neb) basket
nm (*nem) knife

nn (*nen) two rushes
nḥ (*neh) guinea-fowl
ns (*nes) tongue
nḏ (*nedj) ?
rw (*rew) lion
ḥꜣ (*ha) papyrus
ḥm (*hem) well
ḥn (*hen) herb
ḥr (*her) face
ḥs (*hes) water-pot
ḥḏ (*hedj) mace
ḫꜣ (*kha) lotus
ḫꜥ (*kha) sun behind a hill
ḫw (*khu) arm holding a flagellum
ḫt (*khet) branch
ẖꜣ (*kha) fish
ẖn (*khen) arms rowing
ẖn (*khen) goat skin

The most frequent hieroglyphic signs.

Biliteral signs (continued)

- *ḫr* (*kher) butcher's block
- *sꜣ* (*sa) hobble for cattle
- *sꜣ* (*sa) goose
- *sꜣ* (*sa) lid of a quiver
- *sw* (*su) a plant
- *sn* (*sen) spear-head
- *sk* (*sek) hank of fibre
- *st* (*set) hide and arrow
- *šꜣ* (*sha) pool with lotuses

- *šn* (*shen) loop of cord
- *šs* (*shes) loop of cord
- *šd* (*shed) water-skin
- *qd* (*ked) a tool
- *kꜣ* (*ka) arms
- *kp* (*kep) censer
- *km* (*kem) crocodile skin
- *gm* (*gem) black ibis
- *gs* (*ges) ?

- *tꜣ* (*ta) potter's kiln
- *tỉ* (*ti) pestle
- *tm* (*tm) sledge
- *ṯꜣ* (*tja) chick
- *ḏꜣ* (*dja) fire-drill
- *ḏw* (*djew) mountain
- *ḏr* (*djer) bundle of stems
- *ḏd* (*djed) lopped tree

A biliteral sign is often accompanied by one or two alphabetic signs which repeat its consonants but have no value in their own right. It is of the greatest importance to understand this, thus is read only as *ḫꜣ* (*kha), although the signs are *ḫꜣ* + *ꜣ*!

Part 3: Triliteral signs

Some hieroglyphic signs represent a combination of three consonants. These are called triliteral signs.

- *ꜥnḫ* (*ankh) sandal-strap
- *wꜣḥ* (*wah) hank of fibre
- *nfr* (*nefer) heart and windpipe
- *mnḫ* (*menekh) chisel
- *ḫnm* (*khnem) stone jug
- *tỉw* (*tiw) or *tyw* (*teyu) buzzard

Just like the biliteral signs, also triliteral signs can be accompanied by other signs. These help to establish the correct reading of the sign, but have no independent value: is read as *nfr* (*nefer) although the signs are *nfr* + *f* + *r*.

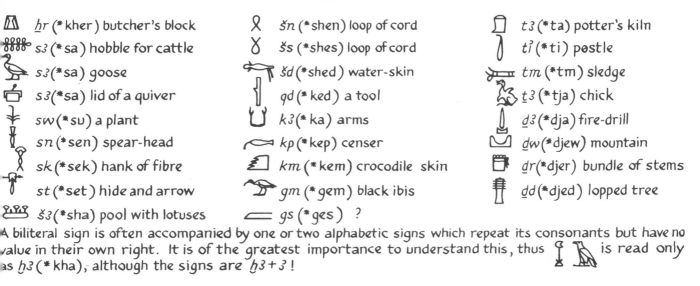

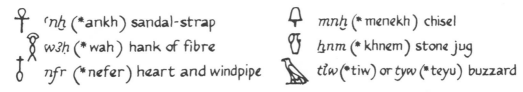

The most frequent hieroglyphic signs.

Part 4: Ideograms

These are hieroglyphs which convey the meaning of the word by representing the actual object or one closely associated with it. This is usually indicated by an addition of a short vertical stroke.

msḏr (*mesedjer) 'ear' | *s* (*es) 'man'
nỉwt (*niwet) 'town' | *t3* (*ta) 'land'
ḥtp (*hetep) 'altar' | *ḏw* (*djew) 'mountain'

Ideograms are often accompanied by signs repeating one or more of their consonants in order to avoid confusion : *ṯ3w* (*tjau), 'wind', consists of *ṯ3w* + *w*.

Part 5: Determinatives

These are signs which follow other hieroglyphs and define the category of meaning to which the word belongs. This was, in the absence of written vowels, necessary in order to distinguish between words which contained identical consonants; consider the problems we should have in English with a word written just as *pn*. It could be : *p*(a)*n*, *p*(e)*n*, *p*(i)*n*, *p*(u)*n*, (o)*p*(e)*n*, *p*(ai)*n*, *p*(a)*n*(e), *p*(eo)*n*, *p*(i)*n*(e), *p*(o)*n*(y) *p*(u)*n*(y), (o)*p*(i)*n*(e), *p*(aea)*n*, *p*(eo)*n*(y), *p*(ia)*n*(o), etc.

man
woman
people
juvenile
old man, old
official
deceased

or or god, king
high, to rejoice
to adore
or force, to strike
to carry, work
tired
or enemy

sleep, death
mummy, likeness
head
hair, mourning
actions of the mouth
actions of the eye
actions of the nose

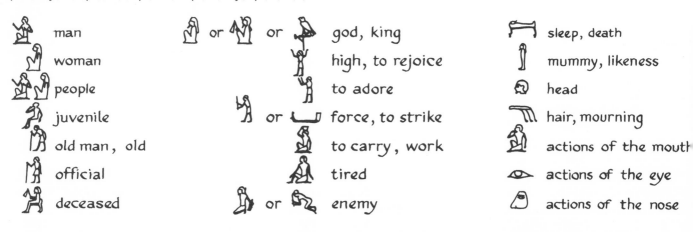

The most frequent hieroglyphic signs

Determinatives (continued)

- actions of the ear
- actions of the teeth
- to offer
- to cease
- to embrace
- negative, not
- to beget
- leg, foot
- to walk
- to return
- limb, flesh
- illness
- cattle
- animal
- bird
- small, poor, bad
- fish
- snake, worm
- tree

- plant
- fruit
- wood
- corn
- or grain
- sky
- sun, time
- night
- fire, to cook
- air, wind
- stone
- metal
- sand
- water
- canal, pool
- irrigated land
- land
- road, path
- desert, abroad

- foreign
- settlement
- house
- door, to open
- shrine, litter
- boat, to travel by boat
- barque
- cloth, dress
- document
- rope
- knife, to cut
- to cultivate
- to break
- cup
- or vessel, drink, ointment
- or or bread, cake
- festival
- book, abstract concepts

Words and sentences

There is no punctuation in the hieroglyphic script, and the beginning of a new sentence is not indicated, so we have to rely on its syntax (the rules of how Egyptian sentences are usually constructed) and context (the general drift of the meaning). The same is true of individual words in the sentence which, again, are not formally distinguished. Here, however, the determinatives at the end of words are of considerable help.

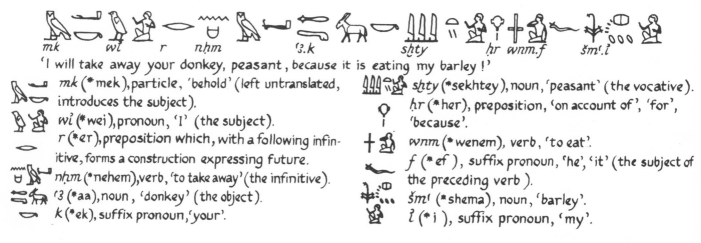

'I will take away your donkey, peasant, because it is eating my barley!'

mk (*mek), particle, 'behold' (left untranslated, introduces the subject).
wỉ (*wei), pronoun, 'I' (the subject).
r (*er), preposition which, with a following infinitive, forms a construction expressing future.
nḥm (*nehem), verb, 'to take away' (the infinitive).
ʿ3 (*aa), noun, 'donkey' (the object).
k (*ek), suffix pronoun, 'your'.

sḫty (*sekhtey), noun, 'peasant' (the vocative).
ḥr (*her), preposition, 'on account of', 'for', 'because'.
wnm (*wenem), verb, 'to eat'.
f (*ef), suffix pronoun, 'he', 'it' (the subject of the preceding verb).
šmʿ (*shema), noun, 'barley'.
ỉ (*i), suffix pronoun, 'my'.

Some grammar

The gender of nouns.

Nouns are either masculine, with no special ending, e.g. *fnd* (*fened), 'nose', or feminine, ending in *t*: *šrt* (*sheret), another word for 'nose', 'nostril'.

The plural of nouns.

The plural ending of masculine nouns is *w*, of feminine nouns *wt*. The plural can be indicated by

1. repeating the noun, particularly when written by a single ideogram, three times:
   pr (*per), 'house', plural *prw* (*peru), 'houses',
   or *nst* (*neset), 'throne', plural *nswt* (*nesut), 'thrones';
2. adding three strokes or three dots:
   prw (*peru), *nswt* (*nesut).

Some grammar (continued)

Nouns and adjectives.

Adjectives follow their nouns and agree with them in gender:

hrw nfr (*heru nefer), 'beautiful day', literally 'day' + 'beautiful';

ḥmt nfrt (*hemet nefert), 'beautiful woman'.

Adjectives also agree with their nouns in number, but this is only rarely shown in writing.

Suffix pronouns.

- *.ỉ* (*i) 'I', 'me', 'my'.
- *.k* (*ek) 'you (man)', 'your'.
- *.ṯ* (*etj) 'you (woman)', 'your'.
- *.f* (*ef) 'he', 'him', 'his'.
- *.s* (*es) 'she', 'her'.
- *.n* (*en) 'we', 'us', 'our'.
- *.ṯn* (*tjen) 'you (plural)', 'your'.
- *.sn* (*sen) 'they', 'them'.

In transliteration (recording the sounds in our alphabet) suffix pronouns are usually attached to the preceding word by a full stop.

Suffixes can be

1. combined with nouns: *pr.f* (*peref), 'his house';
2. added after prepositions: *n.f* (*enef), 'to him';
3. combined with verbs *ḏd.f* (*djedef), 'he says' and similar (*ḏd* *djed, 'to say', 'to speak').

Numerals.

1	*wꜥ* (*wa)	6	*sỉsw* (*sisu)	100	*št* (*shet)
2	*snw* (*senu)	7	*sfḫ* (*sefekh)	1000	*ḫꜣ* (*kha)
3	*ḫmt* (*khemt)	8	*ḫmn* (*khemen)	10,000	*ḏbꜥ* (*djeba)
4	*fdw* (*fedu)	9	*psḏ* (*pesedj)	100,000	*ḥfn* (*hefen)
5	*dỉw* (*diu)	10	*mḏ* (*medj)	1,000,000	*ḥḥ* (*heh)

Example:  13,445

Stela of Sheri

An important part of the tomb of a wealthy Egyptian was a stela with the name and representation of the dead person. The stela was in the chapel which was usually above ground and remained accessible to priests, relatives and visitors after the burial had taken place. The tomb was regarded as the house of the deceased's ka, a concept somewhat similar to our soul. The ka continued to exist after the person's death, and food and drink for it were brought to the tomb and placed in front of the stela. The desired state of affairs after death, with the deceased provided with all manner of goods, is often shown on the stela.

This monument, now quite badly eroded, is the central panel of the stela of the priest Sheri (shown on the left) and his wife Khenteyetka. The couple are seated at a table with offerings (the tall narrow objects on the table are flat loaves of unleavened bread).

No.1836.479. From a tomb at Saqqara. Limestone, height 44 cm. About 2500 BC.

The priest Sheri.

The titles and names of the seated couple are at the top of the stela. A vertical line separates the titles of Sheri, which are written from right to left, from those of his wife, written in the opposite direction. The names follow the titles.

Sheri's first title : 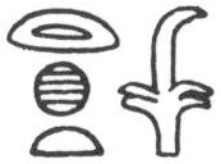

is a biliteral sign *sw* (*su) which represents an abbreviation of *nswt* (*nesut), 'king'. Note the writing of *nswt* which is more economical as well as more pleasing than one which presents signs in their correct order.

could be the preposition *r* (*er), 'to', 'at', 'in respect of', but here it is a shortened writing of the adjective *ỉry* (*irey), 'belonging to', 'concerned with', or 'one belonging to', 'one concerned with'.

ḫt (*khet) means 'affair', 'thing'.

Words such as 'king', 'god', and the names of kings and gods, were usually written before other signs. This is called honorific transposition. Here, the word for 'king' is read last, *ỉry ḫt nswt* (*irey khet nesut), 'one concerned with the affair(s) of the king', although it is the first sign when the title is written down. This was a very common title and meant little more than 'courtier'.

Sheri's second title : 

The frame surrounding the first three signs is called a cartouche and indicates that the name written inside, , belongs to a king or at least a member of the royal family. The king is the rather obscure *Snd* (written *S*+*n*+*d*), Send, who reigned around 2750 B.C.

consists of two words, *nṯr* (*netjer), 'god', and *ḥm* (*hem), 'servant'. Because of honorific transposition the word for 'god' is written first but read second, *ḥm nṯr* (*hem netjer). The combination of these two words can be translated as 'a servant of the god' (the 'god' may refer either to a real god or to a king). 'Of' (the genitive) is understood but not shown in writing.

The name of the king precedes the phrase *ḥm nṯr* in a second case of honorific transposition: *ḥm nṯr Snd* (*hem netjer send), 'a servant of the god Send' = a priest of king Send. This means that although the text is written from right to left, most of the hieroglyphs in Sheri's second title are, in fact, read from left to right!

Sheri's name : 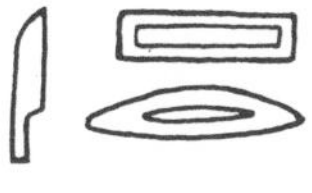

All the three hieroglyphs are alphabetic signs: *Š* + *r* + *ỉ*.

False door of Nemtywer

During the early part of Egyptian history, between *c*.2650 and 2100 BC, the typical tomb stela often resembled a door in an Egyptian house. This was because it was thought of as a symbolic link between the world of the living and the world of the dead. Egyptologists call such monuments false doors.

This is the false door of the man called Nemtywer. Although it is quite crudely made, its design is elaborate. It has two central jambs with a lintel. Above the lintel there is a panel showing the dead person seated at a table (see also page 16). Another pair of jambs and yet another lintel provides the outer frame for the door. Nemtywer is shown standing at the bottom of these jambs.

No.1885.504. From a tomb, probably at Giza. Limestone, height 75 cm. About 2100 BC.

The official Nemtywer.

Nemtywer's name :

In its full form, it is at the bottom of the left inner jamb of the false door:  . The first sign shows a statue of the god Nemty, represented as a hawk, in a ceremonial boat in which the statue used to be brought out of its temple during religious festivals. It is read as *Nmty* (*nemty). The second sign is *wr* (*wer), 'to be great'. The name then is *Nmty-wr* (*nemty-wer), 'The God Nemty is Great'. Egyptian names often were statements about gods. A shortened version, a nickname, appears on the lower lintel and the right inner jamb: and , *Wrỉ* (*weri). The second consonant of *Wr* is repeated; *ỉ* at the end is characteristic of nicknames.

Nemtywer's titles:

These tell us who Nemtywer was, and are on the two outer jambs. The texts are identical, but differently oriented.

The first sign, *m* (*em) could be the preposition 'in', 'at', but here it is a short writing of the adjective *ỉmy* (*imey), 'being in', 'being at', or 'one who is in', 'one who is at'. The second sign, *r* (*er), is the ideogram 'mouth'. The third and fourth signs are read as *sr* (*ser), 'official' (the figure with a staff is the ideogram *sr*, while the preceding sign repeats the first consonant). The whole is then read as *ỉmy-r sr* (*imey-er ser), 'one who is in the mouth of an official', a person who is often talked about, i.e. his superior, 'overseer'. Nemtywer was an 'overseer of official(s)'.

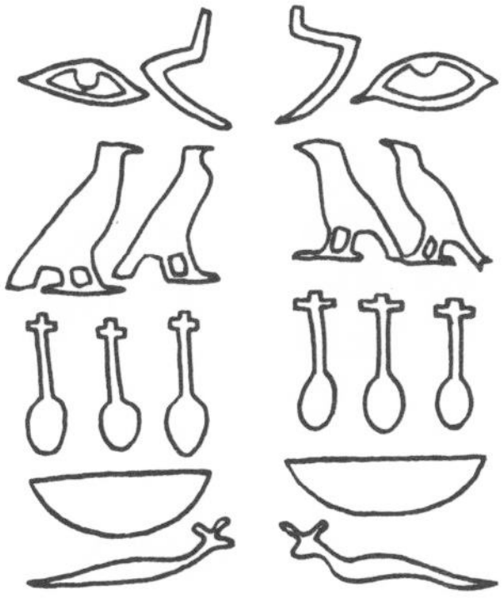

There are four words here. The first four signs are *mꜣꜣ* (* maa), 'one who sees' or 'one who may (or can) see', from the verb 'to see'. The first sign is the biliteral *mꜣ*, the second sign, an eye, is a determinative transferred from the end of the word because of the convenient space, the third sign repeats *ꜣ* already present in *mꜣ*, and the fourth sign supplies the last consonant of *mꜣꜣ*. Each of the three identical signs which follow reads *nfr* (*nefer), but together they convey the notion of multitude or grammatical plural (see page 14) and so can be read as *nfrw* (*nefru), 'beauty'. The word itself is not a plural form – this is just a clever way of writing *nfrw*! The next sign is *nb* (*neb), 'master', 'lord', 'possessor', and the last sign, *f*, is the suffix pronoun 'his' (see page 15). The whole title then is *mꜣꜣ nfrw nb.f*, 'one who sees the beauty of his lord'. It suggests that Nemtywer had access either to the king himself or was allowed to enter the temple of one of the Egyptian gods. The word *nb* can refer either to a king or a god.

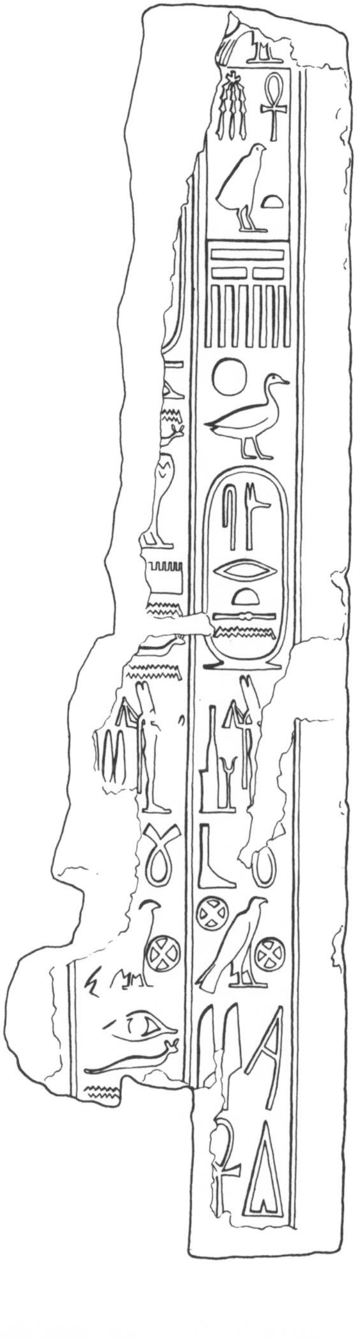

Door jamb of king Senwesret I

On the coronation day, the Egyptian king received his five official names. The following are the names of Senwesret I:

1. The Horus name.

This indicated that the king was regarded as a living form of the god Horus. It is preceded by an image of a hawk and is often written inside a rectangular frame (*serekh*). The Two Ladies and Golden Horus names of Senwesret I were the same as his Horus name.

2. The Two Ladies name.

This associated the king with the goddesses (Ladies) Nekhbet (shown as a vulture) and Wadjit (a cobra). It is preceded by a hieroglyph of these goddesses, placed on two baskets.

3. The Golden Horus name.

This also links the king with the god Horus, shown as a hawk over a sign for gold represented by a golden necklace.

4. The Throne name.

This is preceded by the expression translated as 'the king of Upper and Lower Egypt', the two areas into which the country was traditionally divided. The name was almost always written inside a cartouche. See also page 39.

5. The Son of the God Ra name.

This proclaims the king as the son of the sun god Ra. It was usually also written in a cartouche.

No. 1894.106c. Limestone, height 236 cm. From the temple of the god Min at Qift (Koptos) in southern Egypt. Senwesret I reigned between 1960 and 1916 BC.

The Horus and Son of the God Ra names of Senwesret I.

The Horus name.

It is at the top of the text-column on the right, inside a rectangular frame, with the god Horus as a hawk perched on it (only the legs of the hawk are visible). The name consists of two words. The first hieroglyph ☥ *ʿnḫ* (*ankh), can mean 'life', 'to live', 'the living one', etc. The second word is *mswt* (* meswet), 'creation', 'birth', or even 'image', 'manifestation'. All these meanings are connected with the verb *msỉ* (*mesei), 'to give birth'. The last consonant is *t*, but in order to achieve a more pleasing arrangement of signs it is tucked under the head of the quail chick *w*. The Horus name of king Senwesret I, *ʿnḫ-mswt* (*ankh-meswet) is not easy to translate. Perhaps it means 'The Living One of Creation', in reference to the creation of the world which was thought to have been re-enacted at the beginning of each new reign, or 'The Living One of Manifestations'.

The Son of the God Ra name.

It is introduced by , *sꜣ Rʿ* (*sa ra). The first sign is the biliteral *sꜣ* (* sa), 'son', the second is the ideogram *Rʿ* (*ra), 'the sun god Ra'. 'Of' (the genitive) was not written out. The name is in a cartouche, and consists of three words. Four signs were used for the first word : the triliteral *wsr* (*weser) with *s* and *r* repeated, and finally *t*. The whole word is *Wsrt* (*Wesret), the name of a goddess. The second word, written with only one sign, *s*, means 'man' (it can be more fully written with *s* + an ideogram + a short vertical stroke, as). The third word, *n* (*en), is a short form of the adjective *ny* (*ney), 'belonging to' or simply 'of'. Here, the order of the written hieroglyphs is *Wsrt+s+n* because of honorific transposition, but the name was pronounced *S-n-Wsrt*, Senwesret, 'The Man of the Goddess Wesret'. The king is also known by the Greek form of his name, Sesostris.

The text concludes with 'beloved of the god Min of Qift, given life'.

Exercise 1.

A. The following cartouches contain the names of the famous kings Khufu, Khafra, and Menkaura. Can you recognize which cartouche belongs to whom?

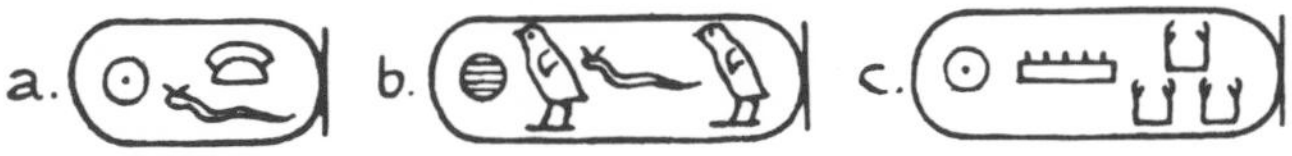

B. What have the pyramids of these three kings in common?

C. Connect the names with the cartouches:
a. *ꜣImn-ḥtp* (*imenhetep, usually called Amenhotep or Amenophis). b. *Snfrw* (*snefru). c. *Nfr-ỉr-kꜣ-Rʿ* (*neferirkara) d. *Ppy* (*pepy) e. *Twt-ʿnḫ-ꜣImn* (*tutankhimen, usually called Tutankhamun).

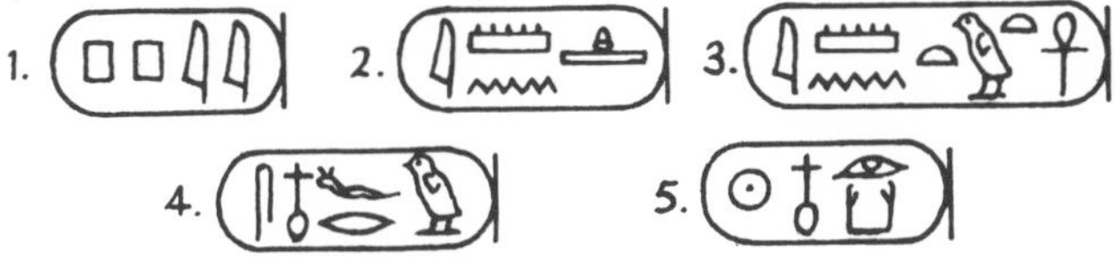

Coffin of Khnemhetep

Many ancient Egyptian monuments displayed in museums were connected with tombs and burials, but this is not because the Egyptians would have been more afraid of dying than we are.

In Egypt, the world of the dead and the world of the living were kept separate. Graves were dug into the dry sand at the desert margins, and tombs were built there of mud-bricks or stone, or cut into the rock. The walls of tombs were decorated with scenes which were either painted or carved into the stone. Statues of the deceased and his family were set up in tombs and various commodities needed for the ka's existence were stored there.

Palaces, offices and houses for the living were built of sun-dried bricks in the narrow Nile valley. When such a structure became too old, it was pulled down and another was put up in its place. Objects and monuments in tombs had, however, a better chance of survival and this explains why so many of them are now in museums.

Coffins were usually placed in underground burial chambers which were sealed and made inaccessible after the funeral. On the outside, the coffins are often inscribed with the name of the deceased person and the offering text (see page 29). The two eyes near the head end of the coffin would have, at least symbolically, made it possible for the dead person to observe the world outside the tomb (see also page 26).

No. 1896-1908 E.3908. Excavated in a tomb at Beni Hasan. Wood, length 208 cm. About 1850 BC.

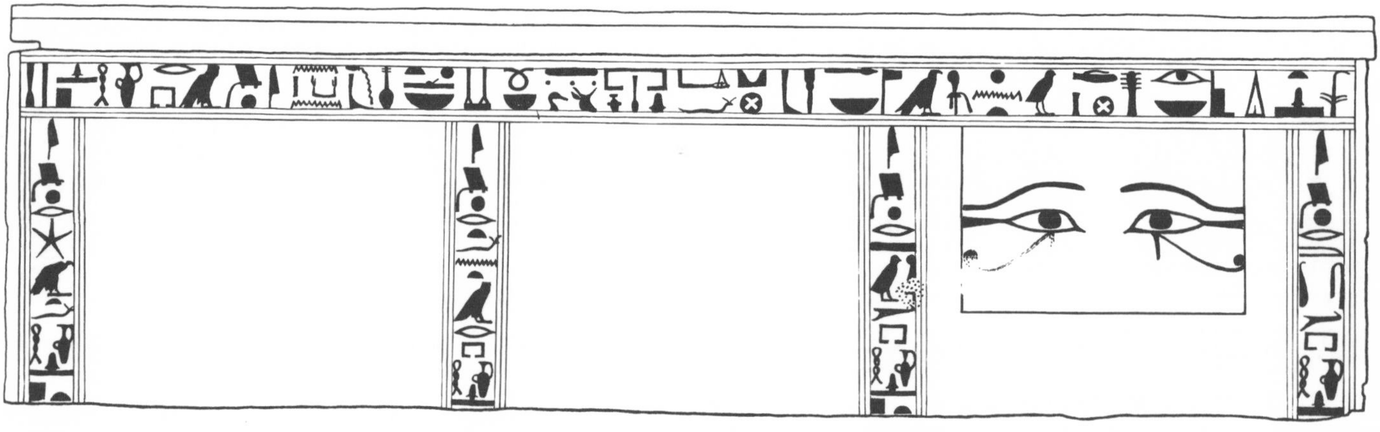

The gods protecting the coffin of the steward Khnemhetep.

Each of the four columns of text on the left side of the coffin starts with the phrase *ỉm3ḫw ḫr* (*imakhu kher). It consists of *ỉ* + *ỉm3ḫ(w)*+*ḫ*+r. The hieroglyph for *ỉm3ḫw* is an ideogram showing a backbone with a spinal cord which was adopted for the writing of the word *ỉm3ḫw*, 'honoured'; *ḫr* (*kher) is the preposition 'by', 'under'. Each text concludes with Khnemhetep's title and name, *ỉmy-r pr Ḫnm(w)-ḥtp* (*imey-er per khnem-hetep), 'the overseer of the house (=steward), Khnemhetep'. The ideogram *pr* (*per), 'house', is written here without the usual short vertical stroke. Note the two variants of the title and . The first is a very clever way of writing *ỉmy-r pr*, 'one who is in the mouth' = overseer (see page 19), by a sign which shows 'what is in the mouth' - a tongue! The name occurs in two variants and . In the latter, the second and third consonants of *ḥtp* are repeated.

The names of deities by whom Khnemhetep was 'honoured' (protected) are inserted in between :

'Imstỉ (*imseti), *'Im+s+tỉ*, 'Imseti', one of the four sons of the god Horus, usually connected with coffins and canopic jars (see pages 46-7).

Šw (*shew), *Š+šw+w*, 'Shu', the god of air. The hieroglyph is a relatively rare biliteral sign.

Tfnt (*tefenet), 'Tefenet', the female companion-goddess of Shu.

Dw3-mwt.f (*dewamutef), *Dw3 + mwt +t+f*, 'Duamutef', another son of Horus. Taken literally, Duamutef's name means 'one who adores (*dw3*) his (*f* = suffix, see page 15) mother (*mwt*).

Exercise 2.

Connect the following personal names with their hieroglyphic forms :

a. *'Ipỉ*, Ipi.
b. *Rn-snb*, Rensenb.
c. *Snb-r-3w*, Seneberaw.
d. *ꜥnḫ-Ptḥ*, Ankh-ptah (honorific transposition! Ptah, or *pteh, was the chief god of the city of Memphis).
e. *ꜥnḫ-K3k3ỉ*, Ankh-kakai (honorific transposition! King Kakai, better known as Neferirkara, reigned between 2435 and 2425 B.C).
f. *Ṯntỉ*, Tjenti.
g. *3ḫt-ḥtp*, Akhet-hetep (*3ḫ*).
h. *'Intỉ*, Inti.
i. *Ptḥ-ḫnw*, Ptah-khenu.
j. *Ḫwfw-mr-nṯrw*, Khufu-mer-netjeru.

1. 
2. 
3. 
4. 
5. 
6. 
7. 
8. 
9. 
10. 

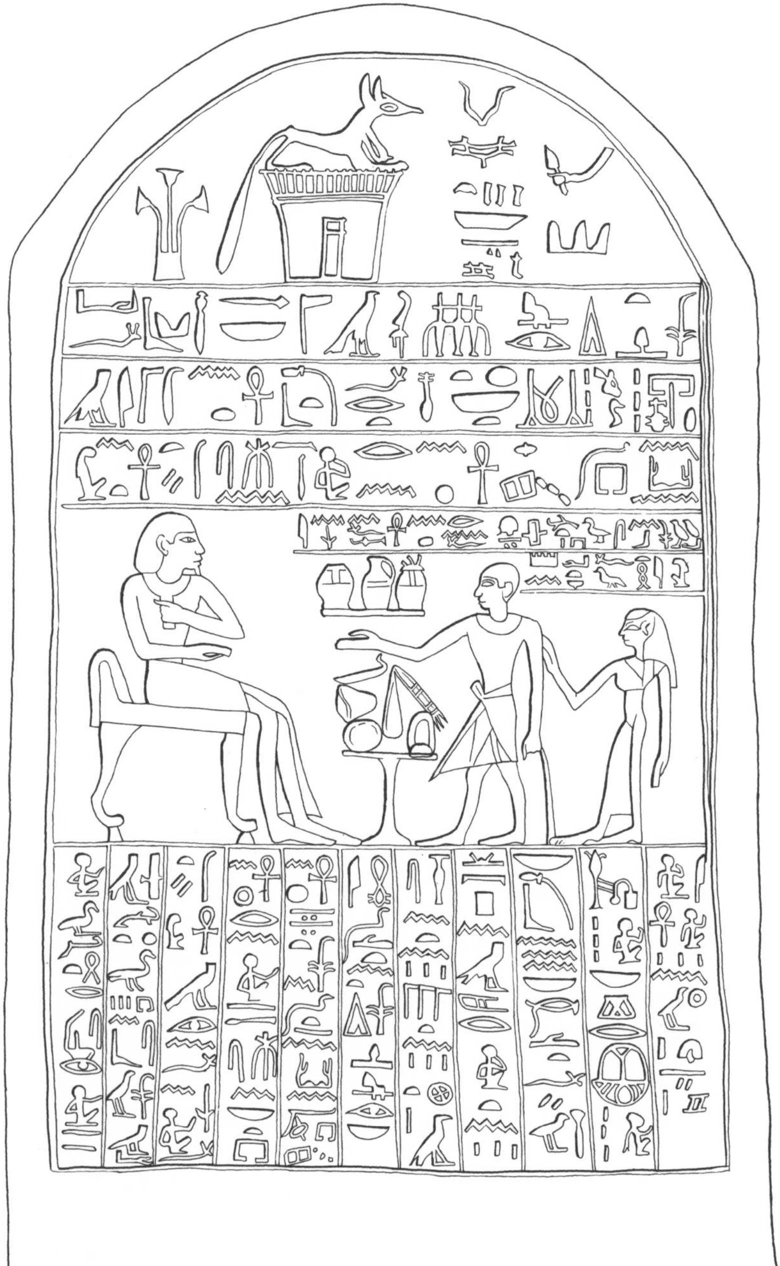

Stela of Ankhreni

Between about 2000 BC and 1550 BC, most Egyptian tomb stelae changed from false doors to round-topped slabs of stone. Their decoration consisted of representations and texts which were usually carved and then painted. The main inscription is the so-called offering text (see page 29) addressed to the god Osiris, the ruler of the underworld, and sometimes also to other deities. In it, the gods are asked to provide various necessities for the ka (soul) of the dead person. Many such stelae come from the large cemetery at Abydos in southern Egypt.

This is a stela of a certain Ankhreni who was an important official in the department of grain accounts. One of the patron gods of the Abydos cemetery is shown at the top of the stela. Below, Ankhreni is seated at a table heaped with offerings, while his brother and sister-in-law are standing before him. They appear to be reciting the text inscribed in the lower half of the stela. The text is an exhortation to people to say an offering formula on behalf of Ankhreni.

No. QC 1113. From a tomb, probably at Abydos. Limestone, height 51 cm. About 1800 BC.

The jackal god of Abydos.

In the rounded upper part of Ankhreni's stela, there is an image of a god in the form of a jackal. The text in front of it is the god's name and description.

The god's name.

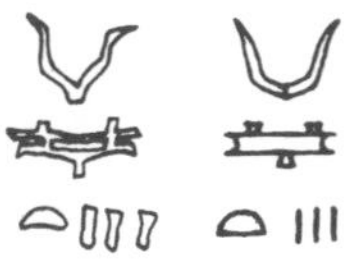

It has two parts: *wp* (*wep), derived from the verb 'to open', here 'one who opens', or 'opener', and *w3wt* (*wawet), 'roads', 'paths', 'ways'. The latter is the plural of *w3t* (*wat), recognizable by the three short strokes (see page 14). The name Wepwawet, 'the opener of ways', is a reference to the scenes in which the jackal god precedes the god Osiris and 'opens the ways' for him.

The god's epithet or description.

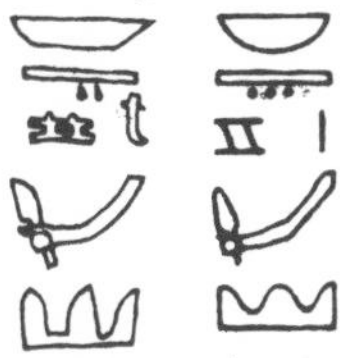

This follows the name, and consists of three words: *nb* (*neb), 'lord' (see page 19), *t3* (*ta), 'land', 'earth' (an ideogram, with the determinative and a short stroke which indicates that the word really means what the sign shows), and the ideogram *ḏsr* (*djeser), 'sacred'. The determinative belongs to the whole phrase *t3-ḏsr*, 'sacred land', meaning 'cemetery', 'necropolis'. The jackal god 'Wepwawet, lord of the sacred land', is often represented on stelae from Abydos and Asyut, both in southern Egypt.

Building up your vocabulary. Part 1.

The following words occur in the columns of text in the lower half of the stela. See page 14 for the explanation of the three strokes.

sš (*sesh), ideogram + determinative, 'scribe'. [2nd column from right].

ẖry-ḥbt (*kherey-hebet), 'lector priest', literally 'one who is under (*ẖry*, *kherey, derived from the preposition *ẖr*, *kher, *ẖr* + *r*, 'below', 'under') the ritual book (written in full as *ḥbt*, *hebet, *ḥ* + *b* + ideogram + *t* + determinative), i.e. 'one who carries the ritual book and reads from it.' [2nd column from right].

wꜥb (*waeb), ideogram + determinative, from the word *wꜥb* which means 'clean', 'pure', 'purified'. [3rd column from right].

Exercise 3.

The name Ankhreni *ꜥnḫ-rn.ỉ*, written with *ꜥnḫ* (a triliteral sign) + *n* + *ḫ* + *r* + *n* + (or), can be translated as 'My Name Lives'. People's names were often exclamations made by the father when the child was born. The word *rn* (*ren) means 'name'. The name Ankhreni occurs on this stela twice. In the first case, the determinative of *rn* is present, but the suffix *ỉ*, 'my' was left out. In the second case, the determinative of *rn* was not written out, but the suffix *ỉ* (see page 15) was. Find these two examples on the stela.

Stela of Reniseneb

Egyptian stelae dated between about 2000 and 1550 BC often show not only the person for whom the stela was made, but also their parents, children, and even grandparents, grandchildren, and other relatives and members of the household.

There are two large eyes, similar to those found on coffins (see page 22), at the top of Reniseneb's stela. He is shown standing in the top row (register), in front of his father Redeysankh who is seated. Reniseneb is holding a censer, an implement which resembles an outstretched arm ending in a hand with a small bowl with incense (the flame rising from the bowl is clearly visible). Purification by burning incense was an important part of rituals performed in tomb chapels in front of the stela. The father Redeysankh is holding a lotus flower to his nose. Another man, scribe Neferimentet, is seated on the right. In the row below, there are (from left): Redeysankh's wife (and presumably Reniseneb's mother) Senebmiu, Reniseneb's wife Nenen, and Redeysankh's mother (Reniseneb's grandmother) Tentetni. Other relatives are represented in the bottom register.

No. QC 1110. From a tomb, probably at Abydos. Limestone, height 48.5 cm. About 1750 BC.

The words describing family relationship.

Reniseneb's stela contains a number of words which describe how the people represented on it are related.

See page 15 for the suffix pronouns which occur frequently.

ỉt.f (*itef) 'his father'; the same writing, , was used for *ỉt* (*it), 'father', as well as *ỉt.f* (*itef), 'his father'.

mwt.f (*mutef), 'his mother'.

or *ḥmt.f* (*hemetef), 'his wife'.

or *s3.f* (*saef) 'his son'; *s3* (*sa), 'son', can be written more fully as .

s3.s (*saes), 'her son'.

s3t.f (*satef), 'his daughter'; *s3t* (*sat) 'daughter', can be written more fully as . See page 14 for the gender of nouns.

s3t.s (*sates), 'her daughter'.

sn.f n mwt.f (*senef en mutef), 'his maternal half-brother'; *sn.f* (*senef), 'his brother' + *n* (*en) (really *ny*, the adjective mentioned on page 21), 'of'. Note that *n* is written as a mere —— on this stela and several other monuments in this book.

Building up your vocabulary. Part 2.

or *3pd* (*aped), 'bird' or 'fowl'. [Pages 18 panel, 22 horizontal text, 24 second line, 26 second line]

, more fully *'Inpw* (*inpu), 'god Anubis'. [Page 18 on the inner jambs]

ỉrp (*irep), 'wine'. [Page 16 above the table]

ỉšd (*ished), 'fruit of the *ished* tree (botanically Balanites aegyptica)'. [Page 16 above the table]

wꜥḥ (*wah), 'carob bean'. [Page 16 above the table]

mỉtrt (*mitret), 'noblewoman'. [Page 16 above the wife]

, also just *mnḫt* (*menkhet), 'clothing'. [Pages 16 under the table, 22 horizontal text, 24 second line]

nbs (*nebes) 'fruit of the Christ thorn tree (botanically Zizyphus spina Christi)'. [Page 16 above the table, with a slightly different order of signs]

or just *ḥb* (*heb), 'festival', 'feast'. [Page 18 on the upper lintel]

or or or or or *ḥnqt* (*henket), 'beer'. [Page 16 under the table, 18 panel, 22 horizontal text, 24 second line, 26 second line]

or *sntr* (*senetjer), 'incense'. [Page 16 above the table]

sḫt (*sekhet), 'loaf of bread'. [Page 16 above the table]

or *šs* (*shes), 'alabaster', with the meaning 'alabaster vessels containing precious oils'. [Pages 16 under the table, 18 panel, 22 horizontal text, 24 second line.]

or or *k3* (*ka), 'bull', 'ox'. [Pages 16 under the table, 18 panel, 22 horizontal text, 24 second line, 26 second line]

or or *t* (*te), 'bread'. [Pages 16 under the table, 18 panel, 22 horizontal text, 24 second line, 26 second line]

Pyramidion of Teti

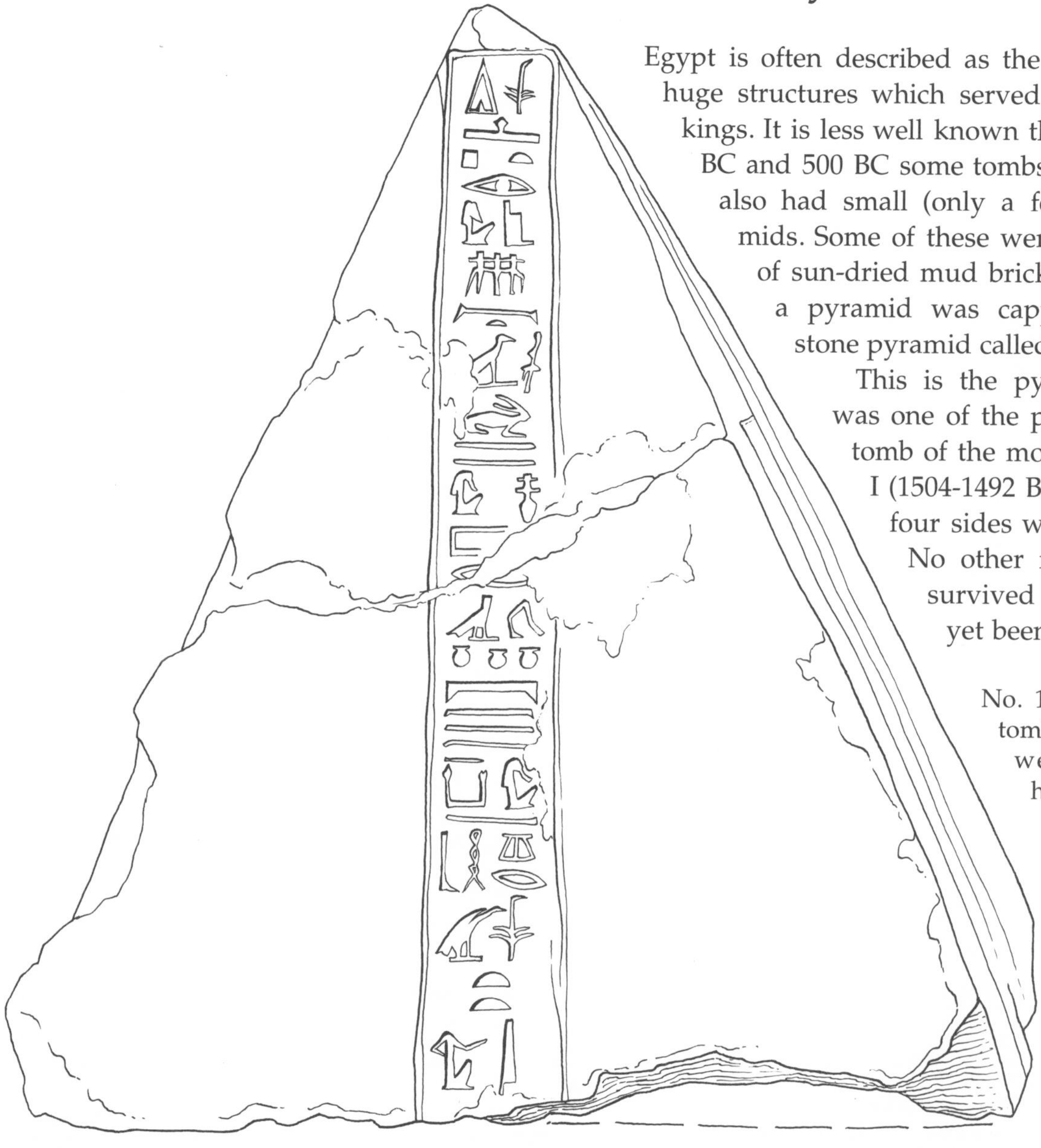

Egypt is often described as the land of the pyramids, huge structures which served as tombs of Egyptian kings. It is less well known that between about 2000 BC and 500 BC some tombs of priests and officials also had small (only a few metres high) pyramids. Some of these were built of stone, others of sun-dried mud bricks. The summit of such a pyramid was capped with a miniature stone pyramid called a pyramidion.

This is the pyramidion of Teti who was one of the priests looking after the tomb of the mother of king Tuthmosis I (1504-1492 BC). It is inscribed on all four sides with short offering texts. No other monument of Teti has survived and his tomb has not yet been found.

No. 1896-1908 E.3926. From a tomb, probably on the Theban west bank. Limestone, height 38.5 cm (measured along the sloping edge). About 1500 BC.

The offering text of the priest Teti.

The most common inscription found on objects connected with tombs is the so-called offering text. It is easy to recognize because it always starts with a combination of the following three words:

or (usually shortened to or), *nswt* (*nesut), 'king' (see page 17).

dỉ or *dy* (*di or *dey), 'to give'. In the offering text this is translated as 'given' or 'may...give!' The verb *dỉ* can also be written as or .

or (usually shortened to), *ḥtp* (*hetep), 'offering' of food or drink. (For another, related, meaning see page 33.)

The text starts with 'An offering which the king gives (to)', or 'May the king give an offering (to)', which is then followed by the names of one or several gods to whom the offering was presented. Then the text may continue with 'so that he/they (suffixes *f*, *ef, or *sn* *sen, see page 15) can give an offering'. On Teti's pyramidion this continuation is left out.

The names of the gods in Teti's offering text are:

Wsỉr (*wesir), 'Osiris'. This is a rather irregular but not uncommon way of writing the name and other forms exist, e.g. (page 24) or (page 36).

Wnn-nfrw (*wenen-nefru), 'Onnophris', another name of Osiris. The last consonant, *w*, is not written out.

The names of the gods may be followed by epithets, short phrases which describe them. On the pyramidion of Teti, the god Osiris is called

ḫnty ỉmntyw (*khentey imenteyu), 'the first of the westerners' (*ỉmntyw* is the plural form of the adjective *ỉmnty*, *imentey, 'western' or 'the westerner', and the last sign is the triliteral *tyw*), referring to the role of the god as the ruler of the inhabitants of the west, i.e. the dead. The Egyptians located the realm of the dead in the west.

The god Onnophris is described as *pr m nnw* (*per em nenu), 'one who has emerged from the primeval waters', a reference to the creation of the world.

At the end of the offering text, there is the phrase *n k3 n* (*en ka en), 'for the ka of' (the first *n* is the preposition 'for', 'to', the second is the short form of the adjective *ny*, 'belonging to', 'of'). The word *k3* (*ka), 'soul', is usually written with a short stroke after *k3*. This is followed by one or more titles of the deceased and his name.

The idea behind the offering text is simple: the king presents offerings to gods and they then share them with the deceased's ka.

The name Teti , followed by the determinative of a seated man, is easy to read. For *ḫry-ḥbt* (*kherey-hebet) see page 25. Here, it is extended by *mwt-nswt* (*mut-nesut), in which *mwt* is read first because of honorific transposition, see page 17. For *mwt* see pages 23 and 27, for *nswt* see page 17. The title then is 'lector priest of the king's mother'.

Queen Nefertiti offering to the sun disc

In the middle of the 14th century BC, king Amenhotep IV abandoned the traditional Egyptian religious beliefs in favour of the worship of the sun disc, the Aten. The king changed his name to Akhenaten (One who is Beneficial to the Aten) and moved his residence to the newly-founded city of Akhetaten (The Horizon of the Aten), modern El-Amarna. Akhenaten was helped by his Queen Nefertiti in his religious revolution.

This is a fragment of a column and it shows Queen Nefertiti presenting a bouquet of flowers to the Aten. The Aten was portrayed as a sun disc with its rays terminating in hands (one of them is touching the protective snake on Nefertiti's crown). The head of a daughter of Nefertiti can be seen behind the Queen.

No. 1893.1-41(71). Excavated at El-Amarna. Limestone, height 34 cm. About 1345 BC.

The name of Queen Nefertiti.

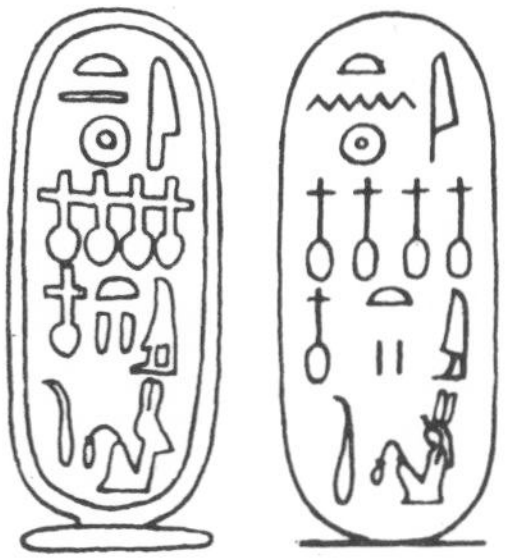

At first only the names of kings were written in cartouches, but later the custom was extended to other members of the royal family. Here, the name of Queen Nefertiti, written in a vertical column at her back, is inside a cartouche.

The first element in the cartouche is the name of the sun disc, the Aten: *ỉtn* (*iten; *aten is a less consistent but better known form). The last hieroglyph is an ideogram, but all the consonants of the word are also written out by uniliteral signs (note that *n* is written by a straight horizontal line). Although the text is in a column and is read from left to right, in the same direction in which the Queen is facing, the word *ỉtn* is written from right to left. The reason for this is interesting. The arrangement ensures that the name of the Aten is facing the same way as the small figure of the Queen (which is a determinative) at the end of the cartouche and so neither of them turns their back on the other! The four identical signs which follow are, in fact, two words. The first, *nfr* (*nefer) means 'beautiful', 'good', etc. The second word, written with another three *nfr* signs is *nfrw* (*nefru), 'beauty' (see page 19). The first part of the name in the cartouche then reads *Nfr-nfrw-Ỉtn* (*nefer-nefru-iten), 'Beautiful is the Beauty of the Aten'.

The first word in the second part of the cartouche is *nfrt* (*nefert), 'beautiful woman', 'beauty'. The second word is *ỉỉtỉ* (*ieitei), a feminine form (the more correct order of signs is , but the two strokes which repeat the consonants of *ỉỉ* were written first in order to achieve a more pleasing arrangement of signs) derived from the verb *ỉỉ* (*iei), 'to come', and means 'has come', referring to a woman. The Queen is usually known by this second part of her name. It means 'A Beauty has Come', and the form which is popularly used is Nefertiti rather than *Nefert-ieitei.

The full name of the Queen then is *Nfr-nfrw-Ỉtn Nfrt-ỉỉtỉ* (*nefer-nefru-iten nefert-ieitei), or Nefernefruaten Nefertiti.

Stela with two cats

Egyptian gods could sometimes appear to people as animals. The cat was at first regarded as a visible form of the sun god Ra, and later of the goddess Bastet.

This small stela contains a prayer addressed to 'the great cat' and the sun god. The texts and representations were not carved but written and sketched in ink which has now faded in places. The two cats in the upper part of the stela represent two different forms of the sun god: the morning sun and the afternoon sun. The god and his visible images, the cats, are asked to be helpful to the couple represented on the stela. The man lifts a small censer with burning incense. His wife carries a copper vase containing water or wine. The monument was probably set up in a local shrine or temple.

No. 1961.232. Probably from a shrine at Deir el-Medina. Limestone, height 21.2 cm. About 1250 BC.

The good cat of the sun god.

The text belonging to the cat on the right reads from left to right, that belonging to the cat on the left reads in the opposite direction. This way, each text is oriented the same way as the animal.

The text on the right starts with the word for cat *mỉỉt* (*miit) (the first sign is the biliteral *mỉ*, the last sign is the determinative used after words for animals). The ending *t* is feminine, suggesting that the word means 'female cat', but these particular cats personify the male sun god. The feminine ending may be due to the fact that at the time when this text was written the ending *t* was no longer pronounced. The next word is the adjective *nfr* (*nefer), 'beautiful', 'good' (the first sign is the triliteral *nfr*, with *f* and *r* repeated). The third word, rather poorly written, is another adjective, *n* (*en) (in full *ny*, *ney), 'belonging to' or simply 'of'. The fourth word, *pꜣ* (*pa), is not easy to see, but it is the definite article, 'the'. The last word, *Rꜥ* (*ra), 'sun god' is written with a sun disc and a stroke to indicate that the intended meaning is the same as the represented object, and there is a determinative of a seated god at the end to show that we should understand this as 'the sun god', not just 'the sun'. The whole phrase then can be translated as 'the good cat of the sun god'.

The second word in the text on the left is *ꜥꜣ* (*aa), 'great' (the first sign is the biliteral *ꜥꜣ*, with *ꜥ* repeated and followed by the determinative for an abstract word). The usual meaning of *ḥtp* (*hetep) is 'to be satisfied', 'to be peaceful' or 'peace'. It is not difficult to see the connection with the word 'offering' (see page 29) – a deity is satisfied or becomes peaceful when supplied with offerings. A little further on, in the third column, *Tm* (*tem), 'Atum' (also *ỉtm*), is the name of the sun in the afternoon (the biliteral *tm* with *t* repeated). For the preposition *m* which occurs in this short text twice, written with two different signs, see page 19.

A cat on a stela
in the Egyptian Museum in Cairo.

Exercise 4.

A. Read the text belonging to the cat on the left. It can be translated as 'the great cat, peaceful in his good name of Atum, in peace'.

B. Why do you think the Egyptian word for a male cat was *mỉỉ* (*mii) or *mỉw* (*miu), and for a female cat *mỉỉt* (*miit)? Such words are called onomatopoeic words.

Papyrus with The Book of the Dead

One of the most important inventions made in ancient Egypt was the writing material known as papyrus. The word, and also our 'paper', probably derives from the Egyptian *pa-per-aa, 'that which belongs to the Pharaoh', perhaps because the manufacture of papyrus was a royal monopoly.

Papyrus was made from the soft pith of the *Cyperus papyrus L.* plant by slicing its stems into narrow strips which were then joined, pressed, dried, and polished. Rolled up sheets of papyrus were used for administrative documents in offices, or were inscribed with religious texts which, it was thought, the dead persons would find useful to have with them in their life after death. One of these compositions is called by Egyptologists The Book of the Dead.

No. 1878.236. Provenance not known. Height 20.5 cm. About 800 BC.

The god Ptah-Sokar-Osiris.

The illustration shows the seated hawk-headed god Ra-Herakhty-Atum. The names and epithets of three other important deities - Ptah, Sokar and Osiris - occur in the text (the second of these names was on the damaged part of the papyrus). These gods were so closely related that sometimes they were regarded as different forms of the same deity.

1. *Ptḥ ꜥꜣ rsy ỉnb nb ꜥnḫ-tꜣwy*, 'Ptah the great, south of the wall, lord of Ankh-tawey'.

Ptḥ 'Ptah', the god of Memphis just south of modern Cairo.

ꜥꜣ (*aa), 'great', see also page 33.

rsy (*resey), 'south', 'southern', 'to be to the south of.' The temple of the god Ptah at Memphis was situated to the south of the city.

ỉnb (*ineb), 'wall' (ideogram). This is a reference to the city of Memphis.

ꜥnḫ-tꜣwy (*ankh-tawey), another name of Memphis. The 'sign' which follows ⊜ is not clear, it could be ⊏═⊐.

2. The second god was Sokar, the patron of the cemeteries at Memphis.

3. *Wsỉr nṯr ꜥꜣ ỉmy Štꜣt*, 'Osiris, the great god who is in Shetat'.

Wsỉr 'Osiris', see page 29.

nṯr (*netjer) see page 17.

nṯr ꜥꜣ (*netjer aa), 'great god'.

ỉmy (*imey) is an adjective 'who is in' or 'who is at', derived from the preposition *m* (*em), 'in', 'at'. It is written with an ideogram, *ỉmy*, and the second consonant is repeated (the same word can also be written with *m* only, see page 19).

Štꜣt (*shetat) or *Štꜣyt* (*shetayet) was the sanctuary of the god Ptah-Sokar-Osiris in the area of ancient Memphis. The sign is the biliteral *tꜣ* (*ta); is a determinative. The horizontal line at the end of this column of text need not be a hieroglyph.

Exercise 5.

Connect the following names of Egyptian gods with their hieroglyphic forms:

a. Amun (in Egyptian *ʾImn*), the god of Thebes.
b. Khons (*Ḫnsw*), a junior god at Thebes.
c. Neith (*Nt*), the goddess of the city of Sais in northern Egypt, often represented with an emblem of two bows tied together on her head.
d. Anubis (*ʾInpw*), the god of cemeteries.
e. Sobek (*Sbk*), the crocodile god worshipped in the Faiyum Oasis.

1.
2.
3.
4.
5.

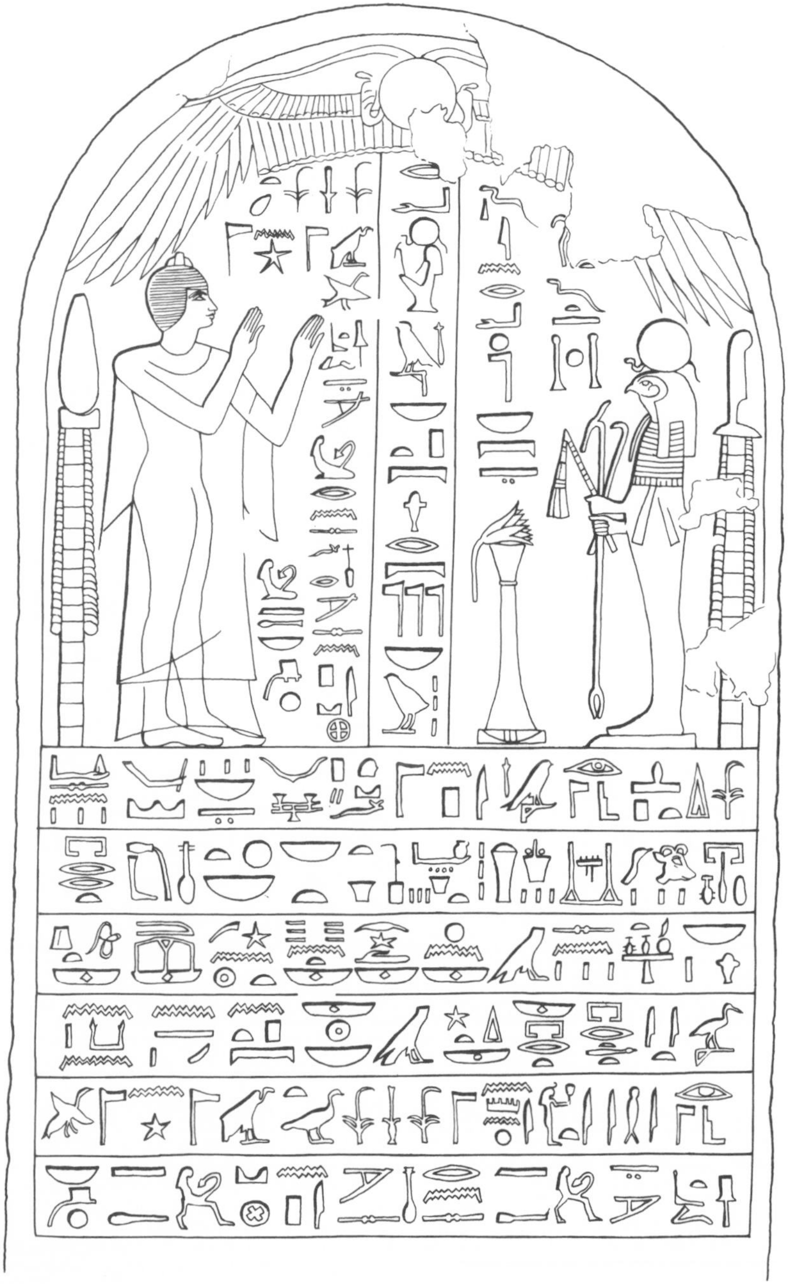

Stela of princess Paabetmer

Egyptian gods were often represented in the form of animals or birds (zoomorphic) or as people with the heads of animals or birds. Animals and birds as such were not worshipped in Egypt, but gods could manifest themselves to people in their forms.

Princess Paabetmer is shown in front of the hawk-headed god Ra; other deities are mentioned in the offering text. The selection of gods addressed in the offering text on a stela was not accidental. Each area had its own god or goddess who played the most important part in the religious life of local people. The choice of the god is a strong clue to the area from which the monument might come. There were also more universal deities, such as Anubis, the god of the cemeteries, and Osiris, the ruler of the underworld; these may occur on stelae from anywhere in Egypt.

No. 1896-1908 E.3922. From the cemetery at Abydos. Limestone, height 90 cm. About 700 BC.

Two forms of the sun god.

The vertical column of text in the centre of the stela belongs to the winged disc above it: *Rʿ nṯr ʿ3 nb pt ḥry nṯrw nbw*, 'Ra, the great god, lord of heaven, one who is over all the gods'.

New words:

nṯr (*netjer), 'god'. The more common writing of this word is (see page 17).

pt (*pet), 'sky', 'heaven'. The Egyptian scribe or sculptor mistakenly reversed the order of the first two signs.

ḥry (*herey), 'being above' or 'one who is above', 'one who is over', an adjective derived from the preposition or *ḥr* (*her), 'on', 'at', with the sign probably added because of its occurrence in the similarly sounding word *ḥrt* (*heret), 'heaven'. Note that appears, also as an ideogram, in a completely different preceding word. The meaning of *ḥry* is comparable to that of *imy-r*, 'overseer' (see page 19).

nṯrw (*netjeru), the plural form (see page 14) of *nṯr* (see above and page 17).

nbw (*nebu), the plural form (see page 14) of *nb* (*neb), 'all', 'every', with the masculine ending *w* written out.

The two short columns of text on the right belong to the hawk-headed sun god Ra: *ḏd-mdw in Rʿ nṯr nb pt t3 ḥq3 ... t ḏt nḥḥ*, 'words spoken by Ra, the god, lord of heaven and earth, the ruler of ... *et*, eternally, for ever.'

New words:

ḏd-mdw (*djed-medu), an idiom (special Egyptian expression), 'words spoken', 'speaking words'.

in (*in), the preposition 'by'.

The correct reading and meaning of this can be established by looking at the following word (see page 25). The words and form a pair of opposites.

ḥq3 (*heka), 'ruler', 'chieftain'. The following word is now almost completely destroyed (only *t* remains), and this is indicated by ...*t* in our transliteration (record of reading) and translation.

ḏt (*djet), 'eternity' or 'eternally'. The last sign, a determinative of land, was probably included because of the similarity with the word , 'estate', 'property'.

a writing of *nḥḥ* (*neheh), 'eternity' (the first sign is the biliteral *nḥ*) or 'for ever'.

Shrine of king Taharka

In the course of its long history, Egypt was on several occasions invaded and occupied by foreign powers. Around 700 BC such an invasion came from the south, from the African kingdom of Kush in the Sudan. The Kushite rulers remained in control of Egypt for more than a hundred years and during this period they enthusiastically embraced Egyptian culture and religion.

The most famous of the Kushite kings was Taharka (also Taharqa) who reigned between 690 and 664 BC. Among Taharka's achievements was the construction of a temple dedicated to the god Amun at Kawa, deep in the Sudan. The small shrine which is in the Ashmolean Museum originally stood in a large columned hall of Taharka's temple. On its exterior walls, Taharka is shown, just like any other Egyptian king, in the presence of various gods.

No. 1936.661. Removed from the temple at Kawa in the Sudan. Sandstone, ground plan 395 by 395 cm, height 230 cm. Between 690 and 664 BC.

On the **east wall** (on your right when standing in front of the entrance):
Taharka offers bread to the god Amun-Ra, the goddess Mut, and the gods Khons and Montju.

On the **west wall** (on your left):
Taharka offers an image of the goddess Maet, bread, and a pectoral to the ram-headed Amun-Ra, and the goddesses Anukis, Satis, and again Anukis.

On the **back wall**:
On the left, Taharka is embraced by the god Ptah. On the right, he receives various symbols from the god Nefertum-Ra-Herakhty and the lion-headed goddess Sakhmet.

King Taharka offers bread to the god Amun-Ra.

This is a museum exercise. Read the texts accompanying the first scene on the east wall of Taharka's shrine (the text below the king's arms says 'offering white bread to his father Amun so that he gives life'.

New words:

ny-swt-bity (*ney-sut-bitey), 'the king of Upper and Lower Egypt' (literally 'he who belongs to the sedge and the bee'). It precedes the Throne name, see page 20 (the fourth name).

nb (*neb), see pages 19 and 25.

tꜣwy (*tawey), the dual (a special grammatical form used for two of anything) of *tꜣ* (*ta), 'the Two Lands', referring to Upper=southern and Lower=northern Egypt. The masculine dual ending was *wy*.

Ḫw-Nfrtm-Rʿ (*khunefertumra), the Throne name (see page 20) of king Taharka, literally 'One Protected by the God Nefertum-Ra'. The verb *ḫwi* (*khui) means 'to protect'. The god Nefertum, here associated with the sun god Ra, was one of the chief deities in the city of Memphis, south of modern Cairo.

sꜣ Rʿ (*sa-ra) and *n* (*en really *ny*, *ney), see page 21.

ẖt (*khet), 'body'.

f (*ef), a suffix, see page 15.

mr.f (*meref), 'his beloved', derived from *mri*, 'to love', and accompanied by a suffix.

King *Thrq* (*Taharka or *Taharqa are the forms of the name commonly used). The biliteral *tꜣ* (*ta), and *rw* (*rew) were used here instead of the alphabetic signs *t* and *r*. This often happened in foreign words or names.

nst (*neset), see page 14. The god Amun (or Amun-Ra) is often described as 'lord of the Throne(s) of the Two Lands'.

di.f (*di-ef), 'he gives', 'so that he gives', etc. (see pages 15 and 29); (or) *di.s* (*di-es), 'she gives', etc.

ʿnḫ (*ankh), see page 21.

wꜣs (*was), 'dominion', 'sovereignty'.

nb (*neb), see page 37.

Mwt (*mut), 'Mut', a goddess usually associated with the god Amun-Ra.

written instead of *nbt* (*nebet), 'mistress'. This is the feminine counterpart of *nb*, see pages 19 and 25.

pt (*pet), see page 37.

Transcription and translation

(above the king, starting with the fourth column from left)

ny-swt-bity nb tꜣwy Ḫw-Nfrtm-Rʿ sꜣ Rʿ n ẖt.f mr.f Thrq

'The King of Upper and Lower Egypt, lord of the Two Lands, Khunefertumra, son of the god Ra of his body, his beloved, Taharka'.

(above the god Amun-Ra)

ʾImn-Rʿ nb nst tꜣwy di.f ʿnḫ wꜣs nb

'Amun-Ra, lord of the Throne of the Two Lands. He gives all life and dominion'.

(above the goddess Mut)

Mwt nbt pt di.s ʿnḫ wꜣs nb

'Mut, mistress of heaven. She gives all life and dominion'.

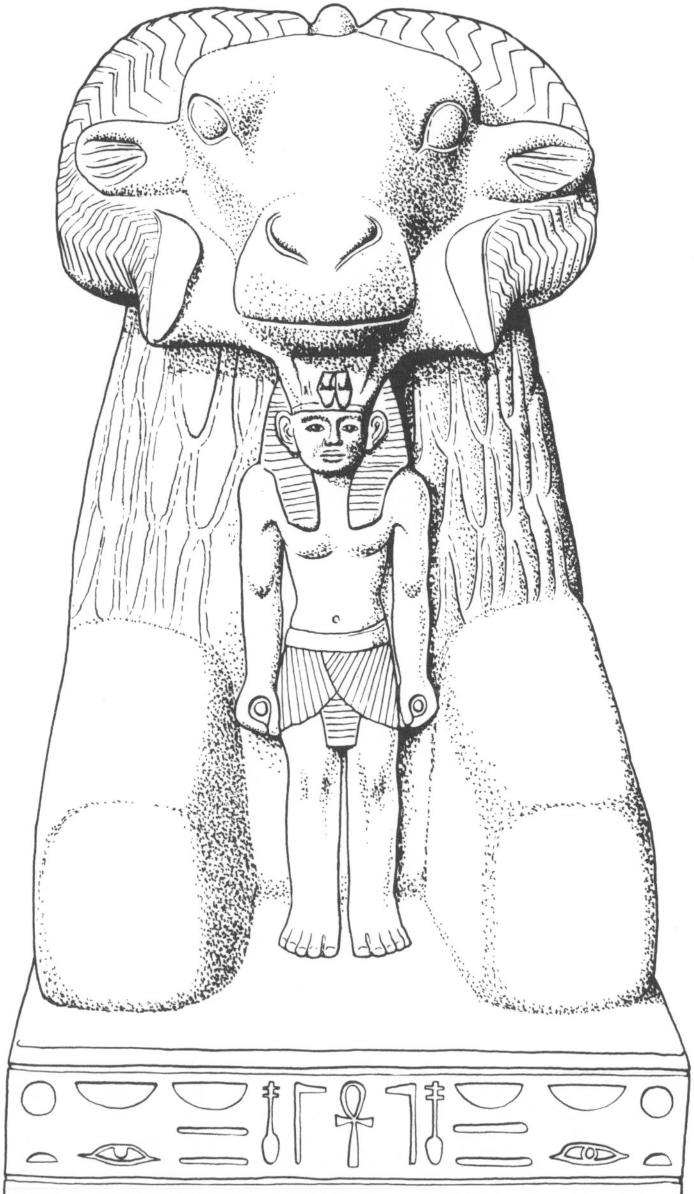

Ram of king Taharka

Around 2000 BC, Amun became the main god of the Egyptian pantheon. At first, his most important sanctuaries were at Thebes (modern Karnak and Luxor), in the southern part of Egypt. Soon, however, temples dedicated to Amun (or the god Amun-Ra who combined the characteristics of Amun and the sun god Ra) began to be built all over Egypt. The god was often represented in a human form, but could also manifest himself as the ram or the goose. It was not unusual to combine a statue of the ram with a small figure of a king. The idea behind this composition was to stress the link between the king and the most important god.

No. 1931.553. Excavated in the temple built by king Taharka (690-664 BC) at Kawa, in the Sudan. Granite, length 156 cm, height 95 cm.

The texts on the ram statue.

The inscriptions on Taharka's ram start at the sign of *ꜥnḫ* (*ankh), 'life', on the front and they run in both directions. Except for the epithet (description) of the god Amun-Ra, they are identical. We shall follow the text which reads from left to right.

(Front)

nṯr nfr nb tꜣwy nb ỉrt ḫt

'The perfect god, lord of the Two Lands, lord of action'.

ỉrt ḫt (*iret khet), 'the doing of things', 'action', a reference to the king's presentation of offerings to gods. In *ỉrt* (an infinitive, functioning as a noun), *t* is not written out.

Dp (*dep) and *P* (*pe), two names of a single important city in northern Egypt, Buto of classical antiquity, modern Tell el-Farain. Note that in our text the determinative applies to both but is written only once. The names of towns are feminine in Egyptian (see page 14) and this explains the presence of ⌓ *t*.

(left side)

sꜣ ỉmn ms n Mwt nbt pt rnn n nbt Dp P ny-swt-bỉty Ḫw-Nfrtm-Rꜥ sꜣ Rꜥ n ẖt.f mr.f Thrq mry ỉmn-Rꜥ nb nst tꜣwy.

'The son of Amun, born of Mut, mistress of heaven, nursed by the mistress of Dep and Pe, the king of Upper and Lower Egypt, Khunefertumra, son of Ra of his body, his beloved, Taharka, beloved of Amun-Ra, lord of the Throne of the Two Lands'.

sꜣ ỉmn (*sa imen) is a case of honorific transposition, so *sꜣ* is read first.

msỉ (*mesei), see page 21. The meaning of *ms n* in this text is 'born of'.

rnn (*renen), 'to nurse'. Here *rnn n* means 'nursed by'.

Note that *mry* (*merey), 'beloved of', written on the back of the statue, is read before *ỉmn-Rꜥ nb nst tꜣwy* because of honorific transposition.

(back)

dy ꜥnḫ mỉ Rꜥ ḏt

'Given life like Ra for ever'.

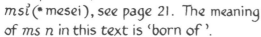

dy (*dey), 'given', from *dỉ* 'to give' (see pages 29 and 39), but 𓇌 *y* is not written out.

mỉ Rꜥ (*mi ra), 'like Ra', again a case of honorific transposition.

ḏt (*djet), see page 37, here with the meaning 'eternally', 'for ever'.

Coffins of Djed-djehuty-iewefankh

It was common in Egypt to place the mummified body of the dead person not just into one but a whole set of sarcophagi and coffins, usually two or three. Around 700 BC a new type of coffin was introduced. It consisted of a rectangular case with four upright posts, one at each corner, and a vaulted lid. Inside the rectangular coffin may have been one or two anthropoid (human-shaped, or more precisely, mummy-shaped) coffins.

This set of coffins belongs to Djed-djehuty-iewefankh who was a priest of the god Montju in Thebes. They were found, together with the rest of Djed-djehuty-iewefankh's funerary equipment, in his tomb at Deir el-Bahri, opposite Luxor.

No. 1895.153, 155-6. From Deir el-Bahri. Wood, length of the outer coffin 216 cm. About 700 BC.

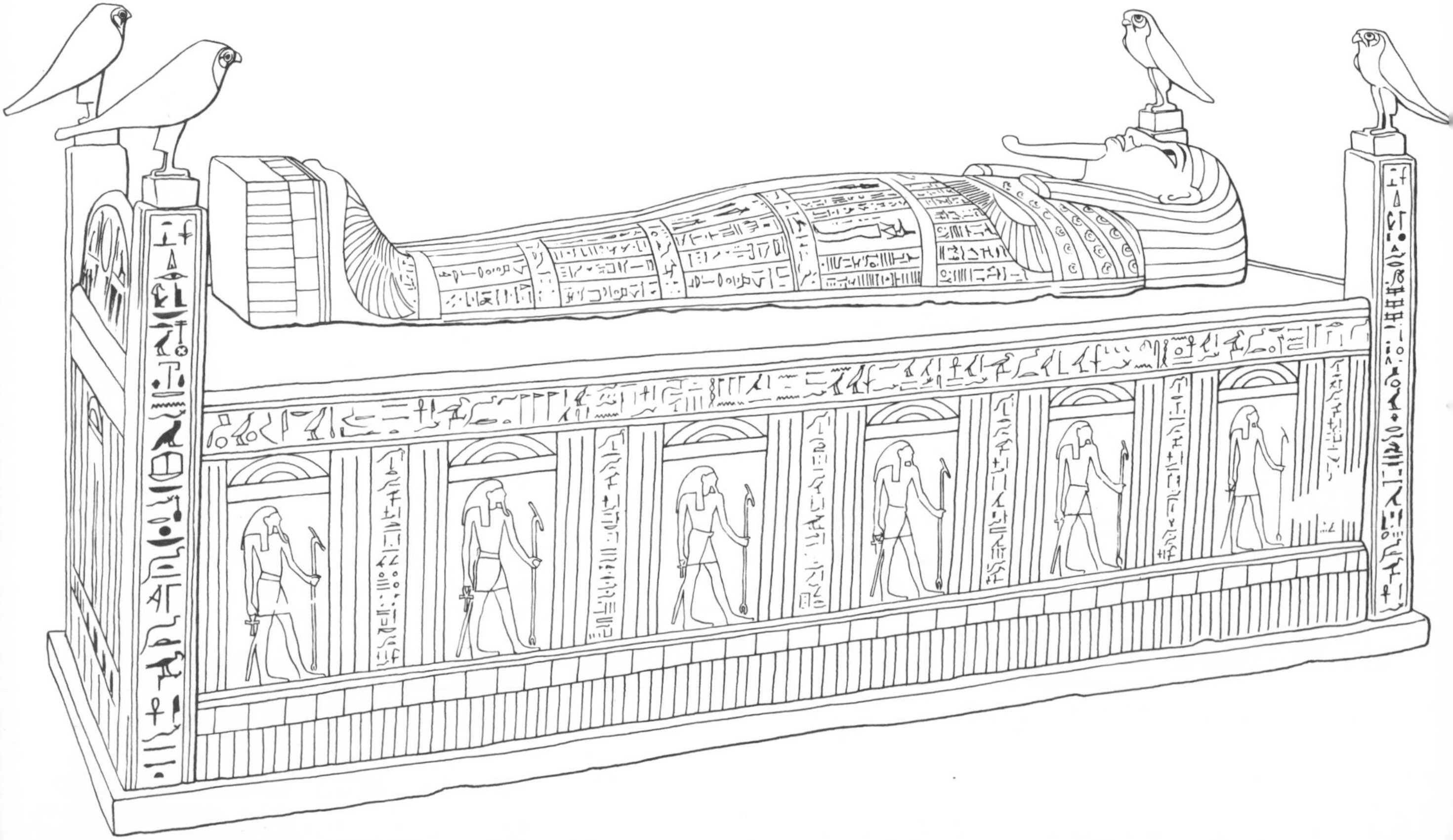

The text on the left post at the foot of the outer coffin of Djed-djehuty-iewefankh.

New words:

Ḏdw (*djedu), 'Busiris', a town in northern Egypt associated with the god Osiris. On page 22, it is written as

prt-ḫrw (*peret-kheru), 'presentation of offerings accompanied by the recitation of appropriate spells'; the expression consists of the word *prt* (*peret), 'the coming forth' of offerings, and *ḫrw* (*kheru), 'voice', referring to the recitation by the priest.

n.f (*enef), 'to him' or 'for him'; *n* is a preposition, *f* is a suffix (see page 15).

m (*em), the preposition 'in' or 'on'.

ḥb (*heb), see page 27.

nfr (*nefer), see page 31.

rꜥ nb (*ra neb), consists of *rꜥ*, 'day' and *nb*, 'every'.

ḏt (*djet), see pages 37, 41.

mr nṯr (*mer netjer), 'one beloved of the god'; for *mr* see pages 39 and 41, for *nṯr* see page 17. This is another example of honorific transposition.

Ḏd-Ḏḥwty-ỉw.f-ꜥnḫ (*Djed-djehuty-iewefankh), the name of the owner of the coffin; it consists of the verb *ḏd* (*djed), 'to speak', 'to say' (see page 37), *Ḏḥwty* (*djehuty), the name of the god Djehuty (Thoth), the god of writing and wisdom, often represented as an ibis or a baboon, and *ỉw.f ꜥnḫ* (*iewefankh), 'he shall live'. The name then means 'The God Djehuty Says that He Shall Live'. Written out in full, *ỉw* would be

mꜣꜥ-ḫrw (*maa-kheru), 'true of voice', consisting of *mꜣꜥ* (*maa), 'true', and the already mentioned *ḫrw* (*kheru), written horizontally. This is a reference to the assessment which everybody had to undergo after death in order to be admitted into the kingdom of Osiris. The sign *t* at the end is superfluous and need not be read.

'An offering which the king gives to Osiris, the lord of Busiris: an offering for him on every good festival, every day, for ever. One beloved of the god, Djed-djehuty-iewefankh, true of voice'.

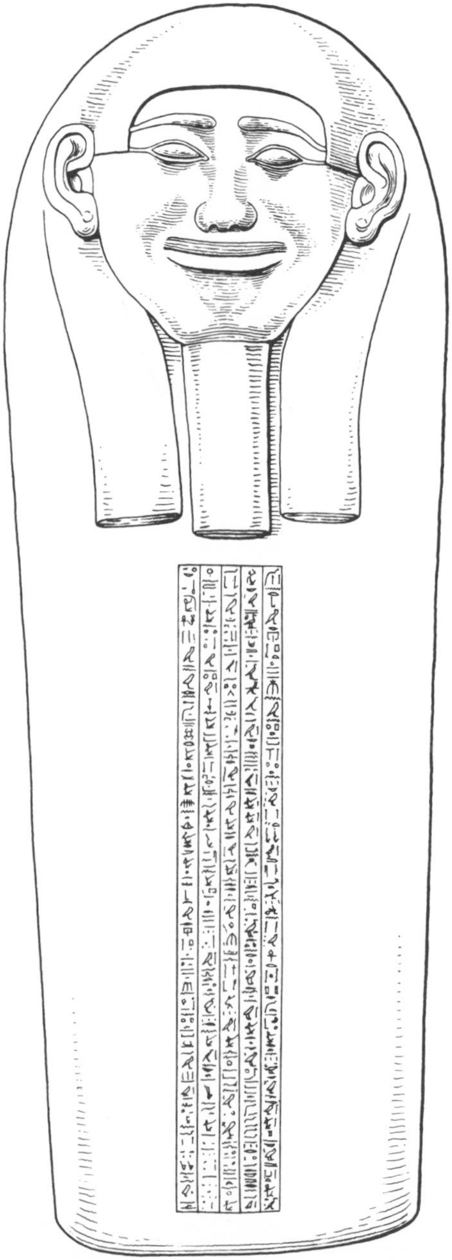

Lid of the sarcophagus of Ptahhetep

From about 1500 BC, many Egyptian sarcophagi (stone coffins) were anthropoid, or human-shaped. They consisted of two halves: a case and a lid. Various types of hard stone, such as granite or basalt, were the preferred material for their manufacture. The mummified body of the dead person did not lie directly in the sarcophagus but was placed first in one or more coffins made of wood or a mixture of linen and plaster (called cartonnage by Egyptologists).

The decoration and inscriptions which were incised on the inside as well as the outside of sarcophagi varied quite considerably. Texts and representations from The Book of the Dead (see page 34) were particularly popular.

The sarcophagus-lid displayed in the Ashmolean belongs to Ptahhetep, an important treasury official. Ptahhetep lived during the rather turbulent period of Egyptian history around 500 BC when the country was occupied by the Persians. He was one of the Egyptians who were prepared to work for the foreign invaders. It is not known what has happened to the rest of the sarcophagus; it may still be buried in Ptahhetep's tomb at Giza. The large tomb which he shared with several other people is situated just to the west of the Great Sphinx, but it is now sanded up and inaccessible.

No. 1947.295. From a tomb at Giza. Greywacke, length 213 cm. About 500 BC.

The names and title of Ptahhetep and his mother.

These are at the beginning of the text, at the top of the first column from the right.

ḏd-mdw ỉn (*djed-medu in), see page 37. This introduces the names and titles.

Wsỉr (*wesir), 'Osiris'. In the later periods of Egyptian history, every deceased person was identified with the god Osiris, so the name Osiris precedes the title and name of Ptahhetep.

ỉmy-r pr-ḥḏ (*imey-er per-hedj), 'overseer of the treasury'. See page 19 for *ỉmy-r*. The state treasury, *pr-ḥḏ* (*per-hedj), is quite literally 'the house of silver' (*pr*='house'; *ḥḏ* = 'silver').

Ptḥ-ḥtp, can be translated as 'The God Ptah is Satisfied'; for *ḥtp* (*hetep) see page 33.

m3ʿ-ḫrw (*maa-kheru), see page 43.

ms n (*mes en), 'born of', a phrase which introduces the name of the mother, see pages 21 and 41.

Ḥr-n-P-t3y.s-nḫt (*Her-en-pe-tayes-nekhet), the name of Ptahhetep's mother which can be translated as 'Horus of the City of Pe is Her Strength.' For *n* (*en) see page 21, for *P* (*pe) see page 41. The word *t3y.s* (*tayes) is another way of expressing 'her' (if written in full, 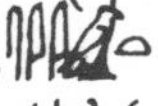 or 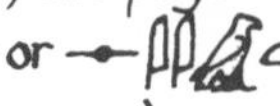) instead of the suffix *s*, see page 15. The word *nḫt* (*nekhet) means 'strength', 'power'.

Building up your vocabulary. Part 3.

 *ḫnty* (*khentey), 'being at the front', 'one who is at the front', 'first'. The feminine form is  or  *ḫntyt* (*khenteyet). This adjective is derived from the preposition  *ḫnt* (*khent), 'in front of'. [Pages 16 name of wife, 22 horizontal text, 24 first line, 28]

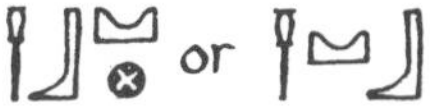 *3bḏw* (*abedju), 'Abydos', a city in southern Egypt. [Pages 22 horizontal text, 24 first line, 26 first line]

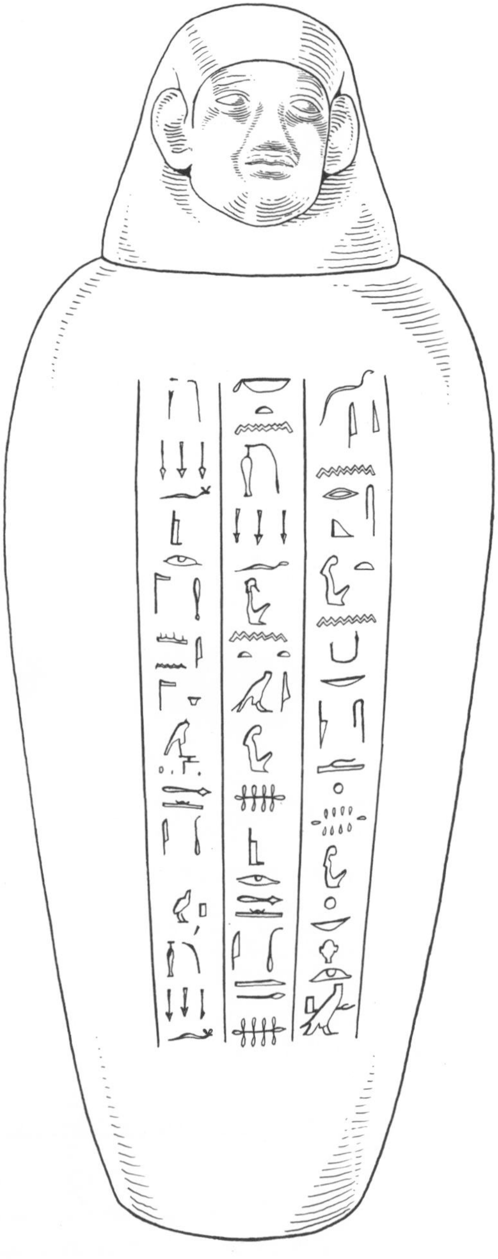

Canopic jar of Aati

The Egyptians believed that the body was required for the continued existence of the ka (soul) after death. This was why from very early times dead people were mummified, preserved by artificial means. The most important part of mummification was dehydration (drying out) of the organic tissues by a naturally occurring chemical substance called natron. This was found in the area to the west of modern Cairo, and in southern Egypt, near El-Kab. When dehydration was completed, the mummified body was treated with various fragrant substances and wrapped up in linen. Also the bodies of some animals, birds, reptiles and fish associated with deities were mummified, but there the procedure was much more basic.

During mummification some internal organs were removed and placed in special containers called canopic jars by Egyptologists. There were four such jars for each burial and they were put in the tomb next to the body of the deceased person. Canopic jars were linked with the deities regarded as sons of the god Horus and had lids of different forms. Each jar and its contents were also thought to have been under the protection of a goddess. The name of the protective goddess is usually found near the beginning of the text inscribed on them, while the name of the appropriate son of Horus occurs at the end of the text. It happens quite often that the lids of the jars get mixed up and end up on the wrong jar.

No. 1879.294. Provenance not known. Alabaster, height 40 cm. About 600 BC.

The canopic jars.

son of Horus	form of the lid	protected by	contents
ỉmstỉ Imseti	man	*3st* Isis	liver
Ḥpy Hepy	baboon	*Nbt-ḥwt* Nephthys	lungs
Dw3-mwt.f Duamutef	jackal	*Nt* Neith	stomach
Qbḥ-snw.f Kebehsenuf	hawk	*Srqt* Serket	intestines

The name of the owner of this jar is *ʿ3tỉ* (* aati). The sign after *ʿ3* is the determinative used after words describing abstract concepts. The basic meaning of *ʿ3* is 'great', 'big', see pages 33 and 35.

Notes:

Isis, Nephthys and Neith are the Greek forms of the names *Aset, *Nebet-hut and *Net.

The first hieroglyph is the rare biliteral sign *3s* (*as).

The name consists of three signs joined, *nb* for *nbt* (* nebet), *t*, and *ḥwt* (*hut).

The last sign is the emblem (ideogram) of the goddess Neith, see page 35.

The sign *sn* repeated three times gives the reading *snw*, see page 14.

The goddess Serket was represented as a woman carrying a scorpion on her head. On this jar, the name is followed by the determinative of a goddess.

Exercise 6.

A. Which son of Horus is connected with this jar? B. What did it originally contain?

C. Which protective goddess is mentioned on this jar? D. What is wrong with the lid of this jar?

Key to Exercises.

Exercise 1: A. a = Khafra; 2 = Khufu; 3 = Menkaura. B. All are at Giza, just to the west of Cairo. C. a2; b4; c5; d1; e3. Exercise 2: a2; b1; c5; d6; e7; f9; g10; h8; i3; j4. Exercise 3: In the 3rd horizontal line and in the 8th vertical column from right; note that the group in the 1st short line in the central part of the stela, *sʿnḫ rn.f*, is not a name. Exercise 4: A. *mỉỉ ʿ3 ḥtpy m rn.f nfr ny Tm m ḥtp*. B. They imitate the cat's mewing. Exercise 5: a3; b1; c5; d4; e2. Exercise 6: A. Kebehsenuf. B. Intestines. C. Serket. D. It does not belong to this jar but to another, connected with Imseti.

Further reading

General information about the Egyptian language and hieroglyphic script.

W. V. Davies, *Egyptian Hieroglyphs*. London: British Museum Publications. 1987. ISBN 0-7141-8063-7.
K.-Th. Zauzich, *Discovering Egyptian Hieroglyphs. A Practical Guide*. London: Thames and Hudson, 1992. ISBN 0-500-27694-3.
H. Wilson, *Understanding Hieroglyphs. A Quick and Simple Guide*. London: Michael O'Mara Books Limited. 1993. ISBN 1-85479-164-8.

Learning Egyptian for complete beginners.

B. Watterson, *Introducing Egyptian Hieroglyphs*. Edinburgh: Scottish Academic Press. 2nd ed. 1993. ISBN 0-7073-0738-4.
B. Watterson, *More about Egyptian Hieroglyphs. A Simplified Grammar of Middle Egyptian*. Edinburgh: Scottish Academic Press. 1985. ISBN 0-7073-0362-1.

How to write hieroglyphs.

H. G. Fischer, *Ancient Egyptian Calligraphy: A Beginner's Guide to Writing Hieroglyphs*. 3rd ed. New York: Metropolitan Museum of Art. 1988. ISBN 0-87099-528-6.

Middle (classical) Egyptian.

Sir Alan Gardiner, *Egyptian Grammar, being an introduction to the study of hieroglyphs*. Oxford: Griffith Institute. 3rd ed. 1957, reprint 1994. ISBN 0-900416-35-1.

Dictionaries.

R. O. Faulkner, *A Concise Dictionary of Middle Egyptian*. Oxford: Griffith Institute. 1972, reprint 1988. ISBN 0-900416-32-7.

Other reading.

P. R. S. Moorey, *Ancient Egypt*. Oxford: Ashmolean Museum. 2nd ed. 1988. ISBN 0-907849-76-8.
R. B. Parkinson, *Voices from Ancient Egypt. An Anthology of Middle Kingdom Writings*. London: British Museum Press. 1991. ISBN 0-7141-0961-4.
S. Quirke, *Who were the Pharaohs? A History of their Names with a List of Cartouches*. London: British Museum Publications. 1990, reprinted 1992. ISBN 0-7141-0955-X.
S. Quirke and J. Spencer (eds.), *The British Museum Book of Ancient Egypt*. London: British Museum Press. 1992. ISBN 0-7141-0965-7.